British D
The 1960s volume One

Dusty Springfield

Helen Shapiro

Cilla Black

Kathy Kirby

David Bret

Copyright David Bret 2016

David Bret has asserted his moral right to be identified as the Author of this Work in accordance with the Copyright Designs and Patents Act 1988. All rights reserved. No part of this publication may be reproduced or transmitted in any form or by any means, electronic or mechanical, including photocopying, recording or any information storage or retrieval system without the permission in writing from David Bret.

A catalogue record for this book is available from the British Library.

ISBN: 978-1539686514

*N'oublie pas….La vie sans amis c'est
Comme un jardin sans fleurs*

Dusty Springfield

Dusty Springfield (1939-99) may well have been Britain's greatest ever female pop star. She certainly was the one who made the biggest impression on the US market, with 18 singles in the *Billboard Hot 100*. The creator of the unique style known as 'blue-eyed soul', she was possessed of a unique, malleable voice—flute-like, powerful, smoky and sensual, frequently in the space of the same song—and was instrumental in introducing Motown to Britain, where in 1964, 1965 and 1968 the *NME* voted her Top British Female Vocalist. Towards the end of her life she made a sensational comeback with the Pet Shop Boys.

   Sadly, this very much larger than life lady succumbed to cancer, weeks short of her sixtieth birthday and on the very day she would have received an OBE from the Queen. Dusty remains a show business legend, despite the brevity of the central part of her career, yet she also remains an enigma, a completely self-fabricated, difficult yet strangely vulnerable woman who allowed few, if any, access into her complex, in turns exuberant and neurotic world where there was at times very little distinction between reality and make-believe.

In an age where being gay or bisexual was tantamount to career suicide, Dusty fought tirelessly to keep her biggest secret, finally coming clean in the 1970s to the *London Evening Standard*'s Ray Connolly:

> A lot of people say I'm bent, and I've heard it so many times that I've almost learned to accept it...I couldn't stand to being thought of as a big butch lady. I know I'm perfectly capable of being swayed by a girl as by a boy. More and more people feel that way, so why shouldn't I?

And that was that—such a fuss over nothing. She was, after all, still the same lovely, much-loved Dusty!

One: Where Am I Going?

She was born Mary Isabel Catherine Bernadette O'Brien on 16 April 1939, in a West Hampstead nursing home, and into a relatively well-off but not entirely stable family. Her tax accountant father, Gerard, had been born and raised in India, but shunted back and forth to Derbyshire for his education. Her mother, Kay (Catherine Anne Ryle) hailed from Dublin, but had been brought up in Tralee. From an early age, Kay had nurtured aspirations to go into the theatre. In 1927, aged 25, she had relocated to London to hopefully realise this ambition, and had at once been indoctrinated into the flapper set. Flappers were radical young things, very much in the stamp of the *demi-mondaines* of turn-of-the-century Paris. They lived life to the full, drank spirits and smoked cigars or cigarettes when it was considered vulgar for women to do so, insulted their peers, painted their lips bright red, bobbed their hair, and casually used 'in words' such as 'divine', 'shit' and 'darling'. They shocked their mothers, guardians and maiden aunts by shedding their inhibitions and their corsets. A young woman who wore her stays publicly was referred to as 'Old Ironsides', and no self-respecting flapper would dream of hanging on to her virginity past the age of twenty. The future Dusty Springfield would inherit many of these traits from her mother.

Needless to say there were fireworks when word of Kay's activities reached her staunchly Catholic parents: though well into her twenties when her father ordered her to ditch her 'dirty' life and start searching for a suitable husband, she dared not oppose him, though it had taken her until the age of thirty-one to settle for shy and retiring Scotsman Gerard O'Brien, five years her junior and the very antithesis of the loud, anything-goes Kay. Neither was it by all accounts a happy union. Like many ex-Colonials, O.B. as he was more familiarly known, had had it bred into him that a woman's place was in the home, and that she should follow the rules he installed within that home. This discipline, accompanied by physical violence, would subsequently be exercised over his family—the O'Brien's had a son, Dion, born in 1934—and frequently involved application of O.B.'s belt or the back of his hand. Even so there were lighter moments, such as the occasional musical soiree when the O'Briens gathered around the piano—with the classically-trained O.B., or child prodigy Dion tinkling the ivories and Mary playing the 'maraccas' courtesy of a box of dried peas—entertaining the neighbours, who earlier in the day may have been treated to one of their frequent rows, which at their most vociferous could be heard at the other end of the street. In August 1985—although this was not the real reason for her remaining single—Dusty told Jean Rook of the *Daily Express*:

> You want to know why I'm not married? I suppose because my parents didn't get on. My father was an income tax consultant who wanted to be a concert pianist—a very bitter man with a foul temper. By the time I was at school my mother thought he was repulsive. I can't remember a thing about my room at home except the raised voices coming from the next door room—the intense bitterness. I'd feel embarrassed to go out with my parents because the arguments still continued. I never invited friends home because I cringed about the rows. I thought, if I married, I would repeat their performance.

Home for the O'Brien's at the time of Mary's birth was a five-floor house at 97 Lauderdale Mansions—although they moved around so frequently over the course of the next few years that it becomes near impossible to keep track: from Maida Vale's opulent Sumatra Road, to a pub basement in High Wycombe to escape the Blitz, then back to the hustle-bustle of London. And eternally rowing, surviving a hellish marriage not at all uncommon to many of their generation. It was a case of one making one's bed and lying on it, with divorce never being an option no matter how dire the circumstances, unless one wished to be regarded as the family or parish pariah. For the rest of their lives Gerard and Kay O'Brien would fight and throw things at each other, but never quite get around to calling it quits.

From an early age, Mary O'Brien acquired the name Dusty—it is believed on account of her then tightly-curled red hair and tomboyish mien which in school photographs reveals her looking exceedingly butch, a far cry from the beautiful, sophisticated creature a few years down the line. Much of her childhood was spent cowering in her brother's shadow. Dion was the firm family favourite and could do no wrong: good-looking, robust, bright and confident whilst she was dumpy, plain and bespectacled, and prone to every childhood ailment. Whilst he was praised for the slightest achievement, she was persistently reminded that she would never be as good as him, instilling within her an instability—and an element of self-loathing—which stayed with her for the rest of her life. As such, in adulthood she would frequently recount wildly contrasting versions of the same anecdote which nevertheless always pointed to the fact that she had been a desperately unhappy child.

There were also far too many childhood bumps and bruises, and the question must be asked as to how many of these were genuine accidents, and how many the result of parental or self-abuse. She certainly seems to have gone out of her way to gain her parents' affection.

'Because I was *so* unhappy as a kid,' she told Jean Rook in August 1985, 'I used to go into corner and cling to the hot water pipes in my bedroom until they were cold, to prove I really existed.'

She also strongly believed in the theory that the apple rarely fell far from the tree, telling the *London Evening Standard*'s Ray Connolly on the eve of her thirtieth birthday, 'I don't know whether I want children or not. The urge to reproduce is always there, of course, but then I think "what for?" I probably wouldn't be a good mother. It would be great spasmodic moods of affection which don't last.'

Dusty also maintained that she had never once seen her parents hug or kiss. Little wonder then that she grew up despising many, trusting few—a tetchy, difficult woman always on her guard, terrified of letting go and revealing her true self. Like David Bowie, Dalida (of whom more later) and Morrissey, Dusty Springfield completely reinvented herself, weaving a web of fantasies, half-truths and foibles about her persona so that by the end of the process it becomes impossible to separate the real person from the self-fabricated creation. Throughout her life she constantly switched identities: the creation which as Dusty Springfield craved attention and adoration from behind the footlights, only to retreat once the curtain came down behind the Garboesque facade of Mary O'Brien, the shy creature who went to inordinate lengths to protect the true identity she did not wish the world to see.

The fantasies, daydreams and distractions evolved from Dusty's fascination with glitzy, exotic high-camp Hollywood musicals starring the likes of Carmen Miranda and Maria Montez, vulnerable gay icons of an earlier generation whose tragic lives had been played out in full Pirandelloesque, public glare. One day, she would augment their ranks, becoming along with Judy, Piaf, Marlene and Marilyn one of the great gay icons of the twentieth century. Unaffected by the war—she was only a few months old when it began, six years old when peace was declared—she was not musically enamoured of Forces favourites Vera Lynn and Anne Shelton, as has been stated. Her earliest memories, extant of Miranda and Montez, were of blonde glamour girls June Haver, Betty Grable, and Doris Day. Having inherited her mother's urge to tread the boards, such thoughts clouded her concentration much of the time during her school years. In September 1944 she was enrolled at The Sands Catholic Primary (later St Augustine's) in High Wycombe. In those days, parts of the Buckinghamshire town were a veritable League of Nations: thousands of Irish, Jamaicans, Trinidadians and Poles had settled here to fill vacancies by those men who had left to fight in the war. Needless to say, racial prejudice ran high, though not so far as Dusty was concerned. Her ex-Colonial father may have looked down his nose at these people and dismissed them as underlings, but integrating with such a colourful, joyful crowd introduced Dusty to the black culture she would come to revere as an integral and essential component of her musical sphere.

Because she spent so much time with her head in the clouds, Dusty's parents never expected her to pass her Eleven-plus examination—Dion was a pupil at the town's Royal Grammar—but she did, and in September 1950 moved to St Bernard's Convent School, a charitable institution run by the Daughters of Jesus, and where the Mother Superior was an eccentric lady who smoked a clay pipe. She stayed here until the end of 1951, when the O'Briens returned to London.

Home for the next few years would be West Ealing's Kent Gardens, and a much tougher school, when Dusty was enrolled at St Anne's Convent, a private establishment run by the Sisters of Charity of St Jeanne-Antide. Here, she suffered the penance of a personal path to Calvary. She was made to recite the Catechism every day, and to attend Confession at least once a week—rapped over the knuckles with a ruler by the nuns, and mocked by the other girls if she had no culpabilities to confess, so much so that she began inventing them just to fit in. And while other schools hired charabancs to take their pupils to the seaside, St Anne's organised 'political and debating' outings to the House of Commons, or 'punitive' trips to Lourdes where, upon threat of excommunication, the girls were ordered to stay away from the opposite sex. To add to her suffering, it was at around this time that Dusty became aware of her sexuality, which must have made life unbearable in this over-chaste environment where she never ceased to be reminded of what hell would be like unless she lived an impossibly blemish-free existence. Her secretary, Pat Rhodes, later stated that in her opinion, Dusty actually felt guilty about her sexuality because this went against the teachings of the Church—that to better cope with her inner demons, she became a lapsed Catholic.

At St Anne's, music once more became Dusty's solace, though like sex, unless this involved singing hymns the subject had to be discussed in darkened corners, out of earshot of the nuns. In these days she had a palpable crush on Peggy Lee, who she first saw in a remake of *The Jazz Singer* with Danny Thomas in 1952. Blonde, beautiful and sophisticated, Peggy remains alongside Ella Fitzgerald one of the finest American song stylists to have drawn breath. Her big numbers in the film were Rodgers and Hart's 'Lover' and Cole Porter's 'Just One Of Those Things', but Dusty 'flipped her lid' over lesser-known gems such as Peggy's own composition, 'Where Can I Go Without You?'

A few years from now, Dusty would copy her idol by dying her hair blonde and dropping her voice half a tone (the back-combing would come later still) to sound more like her. Though she once somewhat foolishly boasted that she had achieved greater success than her idol, this was untrue: Peggy Lee had fifteen years of career behind her when Dusty discovered her, and would have a good fifteen more after Dusty had passed her prime. No such songs were on the agenda, however, when she formed a group with two school friends, Jean MacDonald and Angela Patton: singing at friends' houses or at the school on feast days, their set included blues standards from the Billie Holiday and Bessie Smith repertoires, which the nuns frowned upon to such an extent that the trio folded after a couple of months.

Inasmuch as Dusty had surprised her family by passing her Eleven-plus, so she did so again by acquiring four O-levels: English Grammar, French, Geography and History. Despite this, her parents' praise was reserved for Dion, who had just turned twenty-one and landed a well-paid job as a bank clerk. Whenever Dusty addressed visitors to Kent Gardens in accentuated French, Kay or Gerard would remind them that, whatever their daughter had just said, their son could pronounce it better and in *nine* languages. She breathed a huge sigh of relief when, in July 1955, she passed through the gates of St Anne's for the last time. Reasonably well-qualified, she could have pursued any number of career paths, but instead chose to go on the stage. She enrolled with the Jane Campbell Acting Class, a local repertory group whose speciality was Method and mime. Unable to cope with 'psyching' herself up for a role, or being told to open a door when there was no door there, after just two weeks she threw in the towel and got a job in a laundry. The early hours here did not suit her and after less than a month she packed this in and found employment at Bentall's department store. She was fired from here when, whilst filling in for an absent colleague in the toy department, a customer asked her to demonstrate a model railway and she blew every fuse in the building.

Taking a job in a record shop, Dusty developed another crush—on pretty blonde Irish songstress Joan Regan, who had big hits with 'Ricochet' and 'If I Give My Heart To You'. She saw Joan at the Hackney Empire, and whilst she disliked her longish hair—grown so and styled to advertise Drene shampoo on the television—she loved her flouncy, hooped dresses with their many petticoats. She also went to see Eve Boswell and Lita Roza. The latter wore a slinky, hip-hugging purple sheath-dress, and Dusty went to Harrod's sale and spent a week's wages on one such creation. She put this on in the privacy of her bedroom, grabbed a hairbrush, and used this as an imaginary microphone to mime the latest Peggy Lee and Joan Regan hits in front of the mirror. Her parents were not in the least enthusiastic when it came to supporting their daughter's formative career, preferring to focus on their son instead. Dion had recently begun singing folk songs and could be found most evenings performing in the clubs around Sloane Square. His seemingly limitless talents filled Dusty with envy, but she tagged along and in doing so found an outlet for her own introverted talents—introverted because, thus far at home and at school, no matter what she did she was persistently put down. 'I used to get very upset that I wasn't good enough,' she told the *Daily Mail's* Chrissy Iley in 1990, 'The feelings of inadequacy followed me through my life. Now, I'm grateful to my brother because it was he who unwittingly started me off singing. I started because he started, and I wanted to be better than him at *something*.'

Time would prove this to be so. Closing her eyes and pretending that she was back in her bedroom, Dusty started singing one evening in the dressing room and was overheard by the manager: he suggested that she transfer her talent to the stage, the audience liked her, and she left the club with a clutch of bookings for this and other clubs in the area. Her new vocation as a *chanteuse* was however to be short-lived. For one thing, her father made a nuisance of himself, turning up unannounced every evening to ensure that she was behaving herself and not drinking. For another, not content with emulating Doris Day, Joan Regan, Lita Roza and Ruby Murray, she began singing obscure Latin numbers which resulted in audiences chatting loudly whilst she was on stage. This became so bad that the manager paid her up and she left the club in floods of tears, vowing never to face a microphone again. Disillusioned, she continued working at the department store.

Where her parents were concerned, Dusty's clubland failure was a blessing in disguise. Such places, they believed, were only dens of temptation: the demon drink, and predatory men, though she appears to have shown little interest in either. 'Men were mysterious objects rather than people you love, and with who you feel comfortable, so I went in for crushes rather than involvement,' she later told *Woman* magazine. She was still at heart a good Catholic girl who believed that sex before marriage was wrong, and as Kay O'Brien had once seriously considered having her daughter groomed for holy orders, there was not much chance of her being encouraged to fall in love. What Kay had not reckoned with, of course, was the safer bet of being attracted to other girls in that she would never suffer the indignity and shame of falling pregnant.

Salvation came courtesy of Iris Long, aka Riss Chantelle, a former guitarist with the all-female Ivy Benson Band. Along with Lynne Abrams, Chantelle had formed the Lana Sisters—hoping to become the next Beverley or Kaye

Sisters, they had placed an advertisement in *The Stage* for a third contralto member. Dusty replied, claiming that she was resident singer at a piano bar near Victoria Station. Fortunately, Chantelle never checked her credentials: Dusty was one of a dozen girls interviewed, and fit the bill perfectly. The appointment coincided with the O'Brien's relocation to Brighton, and offered Dusty the opportunity to put some space between them—she moved in with Lynne Abrams, who lived with her parents in Hertford.

Dusty's tenure with The Lana Sisters would be brief, but moderately successful. The trio were handled by Eve Taylor, Adam Faith's manager and the future Svengali of Sandie Shaw—a tetchy, difficult individual loathed by her discoveries, but tolerated because she pulled out all the stoppers to get her acts noticed. One of the trio's first engagements was sharing the bill with 18-year-old Faith at the 2i's Coffee Bar, which stood at 59 Old Compton Street (now occupied by the Boulevard Bar) in the heart of Soho.

'The club was the fuse for the UK rock and roll explosion,' Faith recalled, 'A little ground floor cafe with linoleum floors and formica tables, and a battered piano. Everyone expected it to be a nine-day wonder, but all those old-timer agents sitting around in their old timer restaurants, shaking their heads and saying it wouldn't last, they were all proved wrong.'

When Dusty met Adam Faith, a London film-cutter with a curious 'hiccuping glottal' voice, he was fronting a skiffle group, The Worried Men, at the 2i's. After releasing a clutch of failed singles he temporarily abandoned his music career and returned to being Terry Nelhams, film-cutter, though his and Dusty's paths would cross again.

Soon after hiring Dusty, the Lana Sisters signed a record deal with Philip's subsidiary label, Fontana, and released their debut single, 'Chimes Of Arcady'. On the flipside was

Brenda Lee's 'Ring-A-My-Phone'. The A-side, written in 1930 by American ragtime composer Percy Wenrith, had most recently provided a hit for Billy Vaughan. The record got nowhere, but led to an appearance on *6.5 Special*, the UK's very first television magazine for teenagers, founded by Josephine Douglas and Jack Gold and launched in February 1957. Hosted by Pete Murray from the BBC's Riverside Studios, it went out with the kitschy introduction, 'Welcome aboard the *6.5 Special*. We've got almost a hundred cats jumping here, some real cool characters to give us the gas. So, let's get on with it and have a ball!' The Lana Sisters opened the show for some of the big names of the day: Cliff Richard, Johnny Ray, Morecambe & Wise, Mike & Bernie Winters, Slim Whitman, even Nat King Cole. They harmonised well and looked good in their spray-on lamé pants, but were not a patch on the Beverley Sisters with whom they were most often compared. For their one-off performance on *6.5 Special* they sang 'Buzzin'', of which the least said the better. During the spring of 1959, Eve Taylor also secured them a spot on the BBC's short-lived *Drumbeat*, alongside the newly-returned Adam Faith. Whereas he performed the bouncy, 'What Do You Want?', which would rocket to the top of the charts, they opted for the more sophisticated Continental sound with their version of Italian star Mina's million-selling 'Tintarella Di Luna', which they released as a single early in 1960. It was good, but did not sell.

In all, the Lana Sisters released seven singles, including 'A Heart Divided' with up and coming jazz-stylist Kenny Colman. They *almost* made the big time when they recorded 'Seven Little Girls Sitting In The Back Seat', a catchy number which had taken Paul Evans & the Curls to the upper reaches of the US *Billboard* chart. In the UK they were pipped to the post by the Avons, whose cover-version provided one of the year's biggest and some thought most annoying hits.

In December 1959, performing this song, the Lana Sisters guested in *Tommy Steele's Christmas Spectacular*. Effectively, this was Dusty's swansong with the trio, who soon afterwards were voted seventh in the *Melody Maker*'s Top British Vocal Group category. Even after little less than a year with Riss Chantelle and Lynne Abrams, she was convinced that she had much more to offer the entertainment world than a handful of novelty numbers and meaningless little ditties. And she, who had despised her brother Dion for monopolising her parents' attention and affection, now turned to him to move her one step closer to her goal.

The Lana Sisters

Two: The Springfields

Since leaving school, Dion O'Brien had like his sister changed jobs several times. After leaving Lloyds Bank, he had tried his hand at stockbroking, and had eventually joined the Royal Artillery who had subsequently assigned him to the Intelligence Corps as a Russian interpreter. Upon his discharge in 1958, at around the time Dusty joined the Lana Sisters, Tom Springfield—as he was now calling himself—also launched himself on the music scene as one half of a duo, The Kensington Squares. Tom's singing partner was Tim Feild, an ex-Etonian who had served with the Royal Navy: upon his discharge, it has to be said with financial support from his wealthy family, he had hitch-hiked and busked for a whole year across most of the Far East and America. The same age as Tom, as Reshad Feild he would later carve his niche as an acclaimed spiritual teacher and author. The Kensington Squares had soon established themselves on the London folk scene, benefiting from Feilds' travelling experience and Tom's expertise in languages to become a kind of multinational Kingston Trio.

The decision to add a female vocalist to their line-up and follow in the footsteps of The Mudlarks and The Weavers occurred when The Kensington Squares and The Lana Sisters were performing at different venues in Taunton, Somerset. Tom and Feild put the proposition to Dusty, who said that she would think about it: she did not want to leave Riss Chantelle and Lynne Abrams in the lurch. Also she had reservations about spending too much time with Tom, who had not been her favourite person in the world when they had both been living at home, with Tom getting all the praise whilst she had often been treated like a nonentity. 'I felt awful about leaving them,' she later said. 'I kept thinking that they thought I had only used them for experience—though sometimes you *have* to let people down in order to get on.'

Needless to say, the parting of the ways was acrimonious, albeit a necessary one for Dusty, whose musical tastes were far more in keeping with her brother's than those of the Lana Sisters. With Lynn Abrams moving on to other ventures, a few years later Riss Chantelle formed The Chantelles with Sandra Orr and Jay Adams, releasing their debut single, 'I Want That Boy', on Parlophone in 1965. Three years later, they disbanded.

How the name the Springfields came about is not known. Dusty often half-joked that their first rehearsal had taken place in a field on a sunny spring afternoon. Other sources that, glancing at a map of America, Tom commented on how many Springfields there were dotted around—alternatively, that the monicker was the brainchild of their eccentric Welsh manager, Emlyn Griffiths, who emulated comedian Fred Emney by dressing like a toff and wearing a monocle. Griffiths' first move was to book them on a summer tour of the Butlins holiday camps, on a combined salary of £50 a week, along with whatever tips they could make. For four months they travelled up and down the country in a clapped-out Volkswagen camper van, frequently breaking down and hitching lifts from truck drivers to get them and their equipment to their destination.

Much of the time their reception was mixed, primarily because they never quite knew what to sing—folk, pop, Latin or Continental. Their attempts to inject a little sophistication into the proceedings by throwing in the odd Russian, French or Hebrew phrase failed miserably—this was not what was required during 'Pit Week' in Filey! The youngsters in the audience screamed for Tommy Steele and

Cliff Richard, whilst their parents demanded David Whitfield and Ruby Murray. What they got was 'old ham' such as 'Goodnight Irene' and 'Joshua Fit The Battle Of Jericho'—and audiences showed their lack of appreciation by chattering loudly whenever the trio were on the stage.

By the autumn of 1960, and the close of the holiday season, the Springfields were ready to widen their horizons. Emlyn Griffiths landed them on their feet, so to speak, by booking them for a four-week season at The Churchill Club, a society watering-hole in London's Mayfair. Here, performing their unique brand of pop-folk which ranged from American campfire ditties and Continental favourites, they were in their element and proved so popular with the mostly upper-crust clientele that their run was extended four times. Then on the trio accepted temporary demotion, performing on packed variety bills, often as the warm-up act whilst the audience were still talking their seats. They persevered, and in the end their patience paid off when, in April 1961, they were approached by Philips Records' Johnny Franz and offered an audition for a recording contract.

Johnny Franz (1922-77) was a hugely successful record producer who almost exclusively specialised in home-grown talent, for the better part not even interested in conquering the fickle American market. A former office boy in London's Denmark Street—with its music shops and publishers, clubs and street-musicians the British equivalent of Tin Pan Alley—he had gone on to become a club pianist, then a pianist with the legendary George Shearing before moving to Philips in 1954, whence he had accompanied Anne Shelton and produced her chart-topping 'Lay Down Your Arms', famously adding the soldier's marching sound—by getting his assistant to rattle a box of dried peas! Franz had also produced for Frankie Vaughan, Susan Maughan, Marty Wilde, and a very young Shirley Bassey. Later he would triumph with The Walker Brothers, and with Dusty's solo ventures.

For their audition, the Springfields performed material from their Churchill Club programme: American folksy numbers such as 'Gotta Travel On', 'Far Away Places', and 'Dear John', and Tom's tongue-in-cheek arrangement of the Civil War anthem 'Marching Through Georgia'. This had Dusty coming in with a solo refrain, emulating a coquettish Southern belle, and it was this song that Johnny Franz decided would be their debut single. Rush-released in May 1961, it did not chart, but it received sufficient airplay on the BBC's Light Programme—in pre-Independent days, the UK's only easy-listening radio station—to put the Springfields on the map. Shortly after releasing their second single, 'Breakaway', their names figured amongst the *New Musical Express*'s 'Ten Future Attractions' list—a not so very accurate forecast, for of the others only 'Moon River' singer Danny Williams would amount to anything.

'Breakaway' just managed to scrape into the UK Top 30, and led to the Springfields being offered a tour with comedian Charlie Drake. They also performed live on the Light Programme's *Saturday Club* and *Easy Beat*, and guested on television's top-rating *The Benny Hill Show*. Their 'third-time lucky' single, released in time for the 1961 Christmas market, was 'Bambino', a seasonal song, sung in English and Italian. The Springfields' record company boasted that it would rival the song of the same name, released four years earlier by Franco-Italian star Dalida. This was expecting a lot. It reached Number 16 in the charts, but it was not a patch on the Dalida song—which topped the French charts for a staggering 45 weeks, a record which has never been broken.

Dalida (1933-87) was Dusty's nearest European equivalent. Dusty favoured covering American hits, Dalida English ones, with both stars making them their own, no matter sang them first. Both reinvented themselves and, chameleon-like, changed their images each passing season. Dalida started out as the plain and frumpy Yiolande Gigliotti and within a year had transformed herself into a beautiful but very insecure swan. Like Dusty she was impossible to handle at times, driving one husband and two lovers to suicide. Like Dusty, at times she was too fragile to cope with her monstrous success. Like Dusty she would make numerous attempts on her own life, and eventually succeed. Later in Dusty's career, her manager Vic Billings would make repeated demands on her to work with Dalida, as Petula Clark did, but her plans would always fall through at the last moment—such a shame, for together they would have been electrifying. And it was Dalida, ahead of Cliff Richard, who dubbed Dusty 'Le Négresse Blanche'—The White Negress, an appellation she wore with great pride, once telling a journalist, never more seriously, 'I wish I'd been born black!'

'Bambino' could have paved the way for a Continental career, such as the one currently being enjoyed by Petula Clark. On the B-side of their next single, the tiresome 'Goodnight Irene', The Springfields were singing of 'far away places with strange-sounding names,' whilst aside from a visit to Ireland with The Lana Sisters, Dusty had never left the country. Philips, however, were interested in cracking the much more lucrative American market—once the trio had finished promoting their recently released debut album, *Kinda Folksy*.

Though popular with fans and a collector's item today—on the cover, the Springfields look wholesome as apple-pie, with a purple-clad Dusty sitting on front of a conga drum—

the album was a confusing mish-mash, harking back to their recent holiday camps tour when, unable to categorise themselves, they had been unsure what to sing for couldn't-care-less audiences. The harmonising is mostly uneven—the men shout as if in competition with each other to drown out Dusty completely, and some songs are way too heavy on the bongos and conga drum. Unsure whether fans would want to go the whole hog and fork out for the 12-inch, Philips issued the twelve tracks on three 7-inch EPs. The album kicks off with "Wimoweh Mambo"—noisy and cluttered, performed way too fast, and positively awful compared with the far Superior versions by Yma Sumac and Karl Denver. Things improve considerably with 'The Black Hills Of Dakota', from Doris Day's hit movie, *Calamity Jane*, only to degenerate again with the corny 'Row, Row, Row'. 'The Green Leaves Of Summer', Dimitri Tiomkin's sublime theme from *The Alamo* (performed over the credits by The Kingston Trio) offers a few minutes of magnificence before mediocrity beckons once more with 'Silver Dollar' and Irving Gordon's 'Allentown Jail'. Joe Stafford had introduced the latter in 1951, and if her version was not the definitive one, the recent French version by Edith Piaf certainly was—Dusty herself admitted this. Next up is a way over the top 'Lonesome Traveller', followed by a very pleasing 'Dear Hearts And Gentle People'. Sammy Fain had composed this for Bing Crosby, and it is with this type of cosy fireside number that the Springfields truly excelled. 'They Took John Away' and 'Two Brothers', a hammy Civil War song, are scarcely worthy of mention. The album ends on a lamentable note with Olavi Virta's 'Eso Es El Amor', and the trio's mauling of 'Tzena, Tzena, Tzena', Issachar Miron's Yiddish anthem which The Weavers & Gordon Jenkins had recently performed so well.

As had happened with the Lana Sisters, the novelty of working with a trio. and of not being completely independent, soon started to wear off when Dusty realised that the Springfields were not heading in the direction she had hoped for. For one thing, their tastes in music were different. Whereas as Tom and Feild leaned towards the exotic—the maxim being, 'Why speak nine languages if these can't be incorporated into the act?'—Dusty was becoming increasingly magnetised to the black sounds winging their way across the Atlantic. Peggy Lee, Doris Day et all had been shunted aside in her emotions to make way for obscure (at that precise moment in Britain) R & B acts such as The Marvelettes and The Shirelles, all-girl groups from the relatively new Tamla-Motown label, founded in 1958 by a 29-year-old black entrepreneur named Berry Gordy.

Though no one suspected it at the time, the Motown explosion would be massive: what set out with Gordy borrowing $800 from his family to set him up in business would become a multi-million dollar empire and give the world Martha & The Vandellas, The Supremes, The Four Tops, Stevie Wonder, and a host of others. The Marvellettes would enjoy nineteen *Billboard* Top 40 hits in eight years, beginning in 1961 with 'Please Mr Postman', a catchy little ditty which had nevertheless taken five people to write it. The Shirelles, the first all-girl group to have a US Number On—their 'Soldier Boy' knocked Elvis Presley's 'Good Luck Charm' off the top of the charts in 1962—had formed at around the same time as the Lana Sisters. Dusty would have been far happier recording covers of their B-sides than some of the material chosen by Tom Springfield, and this almost certainly contributed towards some of the dissention between them. One only has to study the British charts to realise what the record buying public wanted: Cliff Richard, Helen Shapiro, Adam Faith, Elvis, Billy Fury and Shirley Bassey were riding the crest of an immensely popular wave, and they were not doing this with tosh like 'Swahili Papa'.

Effectively, Dusty's final emulation of Peggy Lee was to copy her bobbed, blonde hair—firstly by dying her own locks exactly the same shade, then by buying a succession of wigs. Some biographers, focusing much of their attention on the negative aspects of Dusty's life, have stated that she affected the change because of self-loathing, the fact that she hated the image which stared back at her in the mirror, but this is not true. Like many Catholic girls (and boys too, if one studies Morrissey's case) who questioned the more profound ethics of their faith, she simply needed some means of alleviating the enforced drudgery of a religion which had taught her every fear known to mankind.

'The more I watched myself on the then black-and-white television, the more alarmed I became,' she said later, 'In monochrome, my red hair looked jet black. It had to go!'

The bobbed hairstyle would give way to the beehive wigs which would make her appear much taller than her 5 feet 2 inches. It was also at this time that she officially became known as Dusty Springfield, though she had been using the name for some time.

Additionally there were well-publicised personality clashes. Dusty, as yet still a minor star, bore all the traces of a prima donna in the making. She refused to handle the suitcases which contained her hooped, multi-layered stage dresses. What else were men for but to fetch and carry for the lady? Similarly, Tom and Tim Feild felt that they were entitled to a little male bonding. Therefore if there was a lengthy wait between trains, Dusty was left baby-sitting the luggage and equipment, in the waiting room or station hall, whilst they headed for the nearest bar. There were heated arguments about television shows, and Dusty's attempts to draw attention to herself not just by dying her hair, but by 'hogging' the camera—something she could not help, for she had always stood between the two men, face-on, as happened with *all* two-male-and-one-female acts. As if attempting to get even for this, Tom also excluded her from press interviews. 'It was this machismo thing,' she told journalist Kris Kirk, 'I was expected to go on stage and sing my little old heart out, and for the rest of the time keep my mouth shut and my opinions to myself.'

Dusty's singing voice was reasonably strong—not super-charged in the Shirley Bassey-Dorothy Squires sense, but exceptionally controlled in the upper register. Her major problem was that she was performing with two men who, on the face of it, were flat and tuneless shouters as opposed to singers. As such, as a result of trying to keep up with them, early in 1962 she was hospitalised for several days with severe throat strain. Effectively, the only break she had from this was when the Springfields appeared on television—for pop groups promoting their latest release, miming was almost always the order of the day until this was outlawed in 1966. Miming was something Dusty had problems at the best of times—like Dalida, some of her lip-synching in filmed clips is dire, and this caused backstage tension. Additionally, there were arguments about society status. Dusty had always considered herself middle class but accepted the fact that, in this helter-skelter world of pop, amendments had to be made to suit one's lifestyle: cheap transport between engagements, tawdry guest-houses with shared bathrooms, snatched meals. This Dusty was willing to accept, and to a certain extent so was Tom. Tim Field does not appear to have wanted to compromise. He came from a wealthy background, and had always been accustomed to life's privileges. Backstreet lodging houses, roadside cafés and greasy spoons were not his style.

The Springfields also had to deal with press speculation that Dusty and the married Feild were having an affair. To a certain extent, Dusty played along with this. The world was yet to discover that she was gay, and in any case she was too busy forging ahead with her career to pay much attention to her love life.

In the May, the Springfields came one step closer to making that all important trip across the Atlantic when they released 'Silver Threads And Golden Needles', Dick Reynolds and Jack Rhodes' bluegrass classic which in future years would be performed by artistes as diverse as Brenda Lee, Dolly Parton and Janis Joplin. The Springfields' reading is delivered in the country-rock' style later championed by Gram Parsons. The record (along with its successor, the awful 'Swahili Papa') bombed in Britain, but topped the Australasian charts. More importantly, issued on the Mercury label it shot into the *Billboard* Top Twenty. The single was followed by an album of the same name, which sold phenomenally well.

Immediately there were calls for the Springfields to record and tour Stateside. This time the move was curbed by escalating problems within trio's camp. In July, shortly after cutting 'Swahili Papa', Tim Feild announced that he was leaving. The official reason was that his wife was seriously ill, and he needed to look after her. Unofficially, Feild is said to have been sick of getting caught up in the middle of the O'Brien siblings' escalating quarrels. He did however agree to hang on until Tom, the mastermind when it came to making major decisions, had found a suitable replacement. As had happened with the Lana Sisters, an advertisement was placed in *The Stage*, and auditions were held in whichever town the Springfields were appearing. Currently they were supporting Bobby Vee. In Coventry, Tom interviewed his friend Michael Longhurst-Pickworth, a 21-year-old singer-songwriter and guitarist who had also been a friend of Eddie Cochran, and who Dusty took an instant dislike to. He and Cochran had appeared on Jack Good's television showcase, *Oh Boy!* On 16 April 1960, Dusty's twenty-first birthday, Cochran had been critically injured when the taxi he had been travelling in had crashed into a lamp-post in Wiltshire—he had died the next day, also aged twenty-one. Soon afterwards, Mike Hurst as he would subsequently call himself, had given up the music business and taken a job selling insurance. Now, he was coaxed back into the limelight, much to Dusty's dismay. Said her later secretary, Pat Rhodes, 'He was very abrasive ....his manner was brash and he didn't blend in so well. When Tim left, the warmth of the music disappeared.'

Mike Hurst's first studio work as a Springfield was the session which produced *Christmas With The Springfields*, a four-track EP which, unusually, was given away free with *Woman's Own* in December 1962. Much more important was the subsequent session which include 'Island Of Dreams'. Tom's own composition and arguably their most celebrated song, they recorded it in October 1962, coupled with the cowboy ditty, 'The Johnson Boys'. Dusty often confessed to disliking it, saying, 'I wince every time I hear it!' Cynics have suggested this was on account of the opening stanza, 'I wander the streets and the gay crowded places,'—particularly a generation later when the word 'gay' had a different meaning, when there was speculation that the phrase alluded to 'cruising' for sex. A catchy, optimistic piece, it opens after a brief harmonica solo and with its for once perfect harmonising and irregular choral backing immediately uplifts the listener, though as happens with many groups (The Smiths and Morrissey, Queen and Freddie Mercury), one's attention is at once drawn to the frontman (or woman!)—in this case Dusty, whereas the other members of the ensemble are relegated to the minor key. The lyrics also bring to the fore the Americanisms she had picked up while listening to her favourite black music, which would crowd her output for the remainder of her career—the '*hah in the skaa*' for 'high in the sky'. The song was immensely popular: it reached Number 5 in the British charts, and stayed in the Top Thirty for almost six months. When the figures were tallied at the end of 1963, only The Beatles had outsold the Springfields.

Coming from the same session as 'Island Of Dreams' was Tom and Clive Westlake's 'Little Boat', which the Springfields were asked to perform in *Just For Fun*, directed by Gordon Flemyng. An enjoyable piece of tosh billed as '*the* big teen musical', this tells of a bunch of teenagers' quest to win the vote, and is worth seeing for the wealth of pop talent from Britain, America and France: familiar names Bobby Vee, Mark Wynter, Kenny Lynch, The Crickets, Johnny Tillotson and Ketty Lester, whilst representing the French *yé-yé* wave were Eddie Mitchell, Richard Anthony, and Sylvie Vartan—the latter, along with Dusty, being the only one who is as much a household name today as she was back then.

While 'Island Of Dreams' was riding high in the charts, Philips were approached by Shelby Singleton, since 1956 the A&R man-turned-producer with Mercury Records, the company's US side-shoot which operated from Nashville, Tennessee. An aficionado of black music, Sheldon had produced Brook Benton's 'Bol Weevil Song', which had reached Number 2 in the *Billboard* chart in 1962. Since then he had enjoyed great success with Roger Miller and Jerry Lee Lewis—in 1969 he would buy out Sun Records, along with its rock and roll back catalogue. Though not a great fan of their music—he had heard the Springfields in London the previous year, but not expressed any desire to meet or sign them then—as would happen with Nana Mouskouri and French rocker Johhny Hallyday (during his formative years, married to Sylvie Vartan) he recognised a neat little money earner when he saw one, and invited the trio to record their next album, *Folk Songs From The Hills,* at his studio.

The Springfields arrived in Nashville just before Christmas, blithely unaware of the working methods here. In England they had recorded only those songs they liked, the ones which had been 'proved' on the tour circuit. Admittedly some of their choices had been poor, but at least they had had a say in the matter. In Nashville, they were instructed to turn up at the studio first thing, where they were handed the sheet music for that day's song which they would be expected to learn, rehearse and record by the end of that day's session. This went on for four weeks. Additionally, they had to contend with surly technicians who resented any artiste who was not home-grown, and insulted by musicians who spent most of the time yelling instead of talking. On the plus side, they got to perform in a few of the smaller clubs, and on local radio.

In retrospect, one gets the impression that someone was taking the Springfields for a ride by getting them to record *Folk Songs FromThe Hills.* Just what was Singleton thinking of? Dusty sounds so out of place that at times she is embarrassing to listen to in a dozen songs which would not have been out of place in *The Beverly Hillbillies* television series. 'Foggy Mountaintop' and Greenback Dollar' are passable, but everything else is instantly forgettable and indeed should be when compared to Dusty's later work. Even the album cover is patronising: Dusty, wearing a tartan dress, is sitting on a straw bale while the men, dressed in striped 'humbug' jackets pose behind her with banjo and guitar.

There was to be a positive aspect of Dusty's first trip to the United States. During a brief stopover in New York, she found time to go shopping—always a favourite pastime—not for clothes, but for records of black artists not yet readily available in British shops. In September 1985 she would tell our mutual acquaintance, *Gay Times*' Kris Kirk, of the revelation which occurred one afternoon while she was strolling past a Times Square record shop:

> The Exciters' *Tell Him* was blasting out. The *attack* in it! It was the most exciting thing I'd ever heard. The only black music I'd heard in England was big-band jazz and Latin music which I loved. But this was a revelation. I copied a lot of black music, though I'd say The Exciters and The Shirelles influenced me more than Motown. But I'd copy them all! One day I woke up wanting to be Dionne Warwick, the next day The Ronettes. It took me some time to find my own style.....

The Exciters (formerly The Marvelettes) were an all-girl-group, a one-hit wonder whose catchy Leiber & Stoller tune reached Number 4 in the *Billboard* chart shortly after the Springfields returned to England. Dusty would one day call lead singer Brenda Reid and thank her for providing her with the catalyst she had needed to turn solo. 'When Dusty talked about this group,' Kris Kirk told me, 'Her eyes lit up like a child who's just discovered she's the sole occupant of Santa's grotto. "That day," she said, "I well and truly saw the light!"'

The seed had been sown for Dusty's solo career, and at exactly the right moment. From a commercial point of view—and money was all that mattered with *every* record company—folk outfits like the Springfields were becoming old-hat. In January 1963 when the trio returned home, The Beatles, heading the Liverpool Invasion, were riding high in the British charts with their second single, 'Please Please Me'. Other big names, the ones who would not last as major stars, but who made their impression while they were here included Brian Poole & The Tremeloes, Gerry & The Pacemakers, Billy J Kramer & The Dakotas—and The Rolling Stones, who would outlast everyone.

Prior to the pop world taking the full force of this explosion, the Springfields recorded 'Say I Won't Be There', Tom's take, in no way related to the original, of 'Au claire de la lune'. The trio performed it on Alan Freeman's *Here Come The Girls* television show, though the attention, hence the title of the show, was more focused on Dusty than on her colleagues. In France, France Inter's José Artur played it on his late night radio show with the erroneous announcement, 'And now, here's the latest offering from Dusty Springfield.' The writing was very definitely on the wall, despite successful lightning tours of Australasia and Europe. To coincide with their dates in Germany, they released an EP containing a German language adaptation of 'Island Of Dreams', but radio stations refused to play it because it included Pete Seeger's 'Sag mir wo die Blumen sind'—this was already regarded as Marlene Dietrich's personal property. In the March, Dusty made her first official 'solo' appearance on the panel of the BBC's *Juke Box Jury*, hosted by David Jacobs. 'Suddenly, Dusty is emerging as an interesting personality,' observed the *New Musical Express*. On 3 July, the Springfields appeared in a royal command performance before the Queen and Prince Philip, at Glasgow's Alhambra Theatre. Topping the bill was Connie Francis. The press reported the trio to be earning in excess of £1,500 a week, a tidy sum for the time.

On 4 October, Dusty co-presented television's latest teenage pop magazine, *Ready, Steady, Go!* Conceived by Rediffusion's Elkan Allen and producer-manager Vicki Wickham, this was geared towards the Mods, flaunting the latest fashion trends each Friday evening following the show's logo, '*The weekend starts here!*' RSG, as it was familiarly known, ran between August 1963 and December 1966. Its regular hosts were Keith Fordyce, and 'groovy chick' Cathy McGowan who transformed giggly, fawning presenting almost into an art form. Topping the bill in this show were The Beatles, and initially the interview went well when she asked Paul McCartney, 'Is it true that you sleep with your eyes open?' Then, through no fault of her own (she was reading the questions from the sheet of paper given to her by the producer) with her clipped accent and shy mien Dusty made a pig's ear of her interview with the forthright, somewhat crude John Lennon. Firstly she asked him if the rumours were true that he had once been shot for scrumping apples. When he affirmed this, she wanted to know if the pock-marks on his face were the result of his injuries. 'No,' he drawled. 'They're scabs!' Lennon then asked to see Dusty's scabs, bringing their pointless repartee to a premature conclusion. 'I think this is where we'd better finish,' she demurely pronounced, 'What are you going to sing next?' Thankfully, her next two interviews for the show were less embarrassing.

In the meantime, the Springfields were pencilled in for the Royal Variety Show, on 4 November at London's Prince of Wales Theatre: topping the bill would be Marlene Dietrich—with The Beatles halfway down the programme.

When producer Val Parnell replaced them in this show with Tommy Steele, by way of compensation he offered them a spot on *Sunday Night At The London Palladium*, broadcast live on 6 October.

Effectively, this would provide the Springfields' with their swansong. They received a standing ovation after 'Island Of Dreams', then when Dusty announced that after tonight they would be disbanding, an audible gasp came from fans in the audience—while those watching at home were equally shocked, although the backstage rumours had persisted for several months. What everyone found bizarre was their choice of farewell number: Woodrie Guthrie's 'So Long It's Been Good To Know You'. This was hardly sentimental stuff, a 'corn-on-the-cob ditty' about moving home to avoid a dust-storm—and halfway through, Dusty burst into tears. Later she claimed that, like a drowning man whose life flashes before his eyes, in the space of a few seconds she had contemplated a very uncertain future.

As will be seen, she had gone to great lengths to stage the event, and the crocodile tears were her way of putting the Springfields behind her so that she could get on with planning the career she knew she merited.

The Springfields

Three: 'La Négresse Blanche'

Dusty's brother Tom claimed that the reason for the Springfields' split was that *he* had forecast the staggering success of The Beatles, with whom no group would ever be able to compete. Therefore it had been preferable to disband while they were ahead. The music press made up their own minds, citing personality clashes. Some years later, Dusty told an Australian journalist, 'A group is an open prison. After a while you get tired of living and working with the same people, and being disciplined at the same time from outside.' She had recently been singled out from the trio and voted Britain's 8th most popular singer in a *Melody Maker* poll, and since the emphasis had been on her for some time, it now seemed prudent that she should want to spread her wings.

Tom went on to become a record producer and, courtesy of his sister who introduced them, a songwriter for The Seekers. His compositions for them included 'A World Of Our Own' and 'The Carnival Is Over', by and large better than anything he had written for the Springfields. With actor co-writer Jim Dale he received an Oscar nomination for 'Georgie Girl', and during the late Sixties released two solo albums. Today he is most remembered for his work with the Australian group and for being Dusty Springfield's brother. Mike Hurst fared considerably better. After a short-lived tenure with The Methods, he began producing for Andrew Oldham and Mickie Most, and discovered Cat Stevens. Amongst the big names he produced were The Troggs, Spencer Davis, and Manfred Mann.

To launch her solo career, Dusty had no shortage of helpers. Absent-minded and unable to do most things for herself, she acquired a secretary-cum-factotum: Pat Barnett (later Rhodes), had worked for Emlyn Griffiths. Johnny Franz was hired as her record producer, Vic Billings as her manager. Tough-talking but with Dusty a gently persuasive man, Billings had formerly booked variety acts for London's New Victoria Theatre before being appointed deputy controller of bandleader Victor Sylvester's dance studios. Currently, he had a small stable of artistes which included Eden Kane, and Paul Raven, who later achieved notoriety as Gary Glitter. Billings would later describe Dusty as the most pessimistic optimist he had ever known—clipping only the bad reviews of her work, and ignoring the good ones—but he would stick with her through thick and thin. He was one of the few people (along with Pat Rhodes and Johnny Franz) capable of calming her down when she was in one of her moods. Ivor Raymonde (1926-90), an actor-musician who had worked with the Springfields and appeared in *Hancock's Half Hour*, and currently employed by the BBC as a musical director, was asked to provide her with a suitable debut song. Collaborating with Mike Hawker, who had written 'Walking Back To Happiness' for Helen Shapiro, he came up with 'I Only Want To Be With You'. The number was completed in a single evening in Raymonde's office at the BBC, and sung to Dusty down the phone at seven the next morning. Or so the press were led to believe.

The whole process was a charade. Dusty had contacted Billings in the summer of 1963 *before* the Springfields' split, and Johnny Franz had agreed to produce her debut single, which she wanted to be a Bacharach-David song. Missouri-born Burt Bacharach had been collaborating with Hal David since 1957, while working as Marlene Dietrich's orchestra leader. Their first hits had been 'The Story Of My Life'—Michael Holliday's signature tune—and Perry Como's 'Magic Moments'. More importantly, where Dusty was concerned, they had composed for rising star Dionne Warwick, who they had originally hired to pitch their work to other artistes until Bacharach, a master of uneven phrasing which adapted well to her unusual voice, realised that Warwick performed them better. Bacharach was not currently interested in composing for Dusty Springfield: Marlene disliked her (though she would soon revise her opinion) because of the Springfields' German language version of 'Where Have All The Flowers Gone?' Dusty therefore focused her attention on the Ivor Raymonde song which she recorded, along with 'Once Upon A Time'—not at the end of October as publicised, but on 27 September at the Olympic Sound Studios nine days *before* The Springfields' split. The next day he had played the finished result to Johnny Franz and Vic Billings—with Tom and Hurst still unaware of what was happening—and within the hour Billings had given instructions for Dusty's name to be added to the playbills for his Pop Extravaganza tour, about to hit the road. She would be sharing equal-billing with Dave Berry & The Cruisers, The Searchers, Brian Poole & The Tremeloes, and Freddie & The Dreamers.

The charade continued when The Springfields were added to the line-up of *It's All Over Town*, directed by Douglas Hickox. Like *Just For Fun*, this was another slice of hokum aimed at promoting the pop stars of the day and selling their records. Co-written by Lance Percival, who headed the credits, the cast included Frankie Vaughan, The Bachelors, The Hollies, and Clodagh Rogers. The film's musical director just happened to be Ivor Raymonde, which gave him and Dusty plenty of opportunities to huddle in corners and discuss her future without arousing suspicion. The Springfields sang both sides of their new single, 'If I Was Down And Out' and 'Maracabamba'—the latter a horror only marginally less dreadful than 'Wimoweh'. The single, released in January 1964, would not surprisingly prove a flop.

For her first solo outing, Dusty asked Johnny Franz to duplicate Phil Spector's trademark 'Wall of Sound', a multi-layered, dense but sometimes slightly tinny effect which sounded good on jukeboxes, but which on account of the technical wizardry involved did not reproduce well on the stage. Spector specialised in black girl-groups, The Ronettes and The Crystals being his biggest success story so far. Dusty was looking for an orchestral backing along the lines of The Crystals' 'Then He Kissed Me'. Ivor Raymonde recorded the orchestrations at the Marble Arch Studios on 23 September, using twenty members of The Royal Philharmonic. He then slightly distorted the acetate to come up with a near-replica of the Spector sound, at a fraction of the cost. A pleasing cacophony of cascading drumrolls, horns and rock guitars, and with an elaborate string-filled middle-section solo, 'I Only Want To Be With You' was released on 8 November 1963. With Dusty's own composition, 'Once Upon A Time', on the flipside it reached Number 4 in the British charts, and peaked at Number 12 on the US *Billboard* chart, earning her a gold disc for sales in excess of a million copies. Unlike most of the early Spector recordings, almost half a century on it does not sound dated, and has fuelled many cover versions ranging from a passable one by Annie Lennox, to a truly lamentable one by *Sun* Page Three Girl, Samantha Fox.

Because she had been a last minute addition to Vic Billings' tour, Dusty had no backing group, therefore when the tour kicked off in Halifax she was accompanied by The

Cruisers. These were able musicians, well-suited to Dave Berry's plaintive vocalising, but what Dusty really needed was 'oomph'—an ensemble which would provide her with the Motown sound she championed. This lack of cohesion robbed her early live solo performances of their magic, and affected her nerves which were never strong at the best of times. She had always suffered from stage fright, but whilst with the Lana Sisters and the Springfields there had always been someone else on stage to guide her through her set. Standing in front of a quartet of strangers made her terrified of forgetting her words and at the back of her mind was the dreading that audiences would laugh at her. This never happened, but each evening ended with her in a bad mood, taking her frustration out of whoever happened to be close at hand—more often than not, Vic Billings. It was he who placed the newspaper advertisements this time, though to be honest it was unfair of him to have added her to the tour in the first place without the requisite musicians.

After several auditions, Dusty settled for The Echoes, who joined the tour in Liverpool shortly before Christmas. Formed in 1959 as Chris Wayne & The Echoes, they had worked with Conway Twitty, Gene Vincent, and Jerry Lee Lewis. After several changes their line-up when they joined Dusty was bassist Douggie Reece, organist Micky Garrett, Peter Clifford on guitar, and Bob Wackett on percussion. Later, The Echoes ranks would be swelled by the addition of trombonist Derek Wadsworth, trumpeter Derek Andrews, and numerous black backing singers. 'The only ones worth having,' she said. Her favourite was Madeleine

Bell, an aficionado of gospel singer Mahalia Jackson who had arrived in Britain in 1962, aged twenty, with the *Black Nativity* gospel revue. Written by gay radical Langston Hughes, this had played on Broadway before touring North America. When Dusty met Madeleine Bell the revue was playing to packed audiences at the Strand Theatre: when it closed and the rest of the troupe headed home, Bell stayed put. Though she was always kindness itself to her backing singers, Dusty could be a martinet where her musicians were concerned, screaming abuse if they messed up an arrangement or hit a wrong note during rehearsals. There were however compensations: later in her career when she was commanding huge fees, she would pay The Echoes more for one performance than they would have earned in a week working for anyone else.

In December 1963, Dusty broke off her tour to travel to Paris. Marlene Dietrich, who had accused her of 'ruining' 'Sag mir wo die Blumen sind', had read of her obsession with Burt Bacharach's music, and invited her to her premiere at the Olympia, then as now the most prestigious music-hall in France. Edith Piaf should have been topping the bill: she had died in October, plunging the country into mourning. The theatre's director, Bruno Coquatrix, had brought in Marlene, Piaf's best friend, well aware that its famously tetchy audiences would never settle for second best. In these days, Marlene never worked anywhere without Bacharach. Three months earlier, she had performed his and Hal David's 'Anyone Who Had A Heart' in one of her recitals—the only time she ever sang it—before handing it over to Bacharach's 'star pupil', Dionne Warwick, whose version would sell a million copies by the end of the year. There would follow several cover versions of the song—the most celebrated by Cilla Black. Marlene had called Warwick, 'The natural successor to Joséphine Baker, a beautiful black pearl,' telling me afterwards, 'Well, I had to say *something* good about her to keep Bacharach on side, though to be honest I thought she was awful!' To placate him—worried that the pop songs would take over and that she would have to look for a new orchestra leader (which is what eventually happened)—she had requested that Warwick be her *vedette-américaine* at the Olympia. This was the artiste secondary to the top of the bill who closed the first half of the programme. This had not been possible: the mime-artiste, Marcel Marceau, had been engaged at the same time as Piaf. Warwick was therefore relegated to performing three songs. Preceding her on the bill was 12-year-old Motown prodigy Little Stevie Wonder, who received a lukewarm reception from the audience.

After the show, Dusty met Marlene. 'I'd heard her singing on the radio, naturally,' she told me some years later. 'But until then I'd assumed she was black. She had that sort of voice and over the years it got better. When Dusty Springfield sang "Ne me quitte pas", it broke your heart.' It was Marlene who introduced her to Burt Bacharach, who promised to write her a song 'very soon'.

Dusty's three-day trip to Paris enabled her to complete her transformation from 'clumsy, red-headed frump' to svelt, sophisticated chanteuse. An avid reader of anything from *Vogue* magazine to the classics, she stopped at a pavement newspaper kiosk and bought every pop, fashion and women's magazine they had. Their covers were graced with the likes of singers Sylvie Vartan, who she had met in London, Juliette Gréco, the darling of the Existentialists whom she met now—and actresses Catherine Deneuve and Delphine Seyrig. She went to see Seyrig's most celebrated film, *Last Year At Marienbad*, and was soon emulating her slinky stance. Vartan, who also later peroxided her hair, she was keen on at the time and she commissioned a bobbed, dark-blonde Vartan-style wig. In 1966, however, she would revise her opinion about the singer when, during the taping of a French pop programme a bunch of Vartan fans who believed her to be imitating their idol began whistling and flicking coins on to the stage—in France, a sign of derision. Dusty also commissioned a lighter-coloured, slightly more bouffant wig which she would wear with a black velvet band, a la Deneuve. Gréco inspired Dusty's choice in heavy mascara and clothes—tight-fitting, ankle-length 'hobble' gowns which she copied. Gréco had always strictly adhered to the *chanteuse-réaliste* tradition of only ever wearing black on stage, whereas Dusty chose pastel colours.

Meanwhile, it was back to touring, promotions, and the final preparations for her debut album. Dusty had recently moved into a flat in London's Baker Street—*Ready, Steady, Go!*'s Vicki Wickham lived in the same building. Vic Billing's and Pat Rhodes' major problem was ensuring that she got to each venue on time. She had bought herself a sports car and insisted on driving herself to the engagement if this was less than fifty miles from home, otherwise the tour bus was kept waiting for hours until her team had got her out of bed and 'in working order'. Though no great party animal, Dusty liked to entertain and often would not get to bed until 4 am, whilst the tour bus usually left its garage near Marylebone Station at eight in the dot. Tempers were therefore often frayed by the time the show hit the road.

On 1 January 1964, the BBC broadcast its very first edition of *Top of the Pops* from its Manchester Rusholm Studios. Introduced by Jimmy Saville, and with the singers miming to their records, Dusty appeared after The Rolling

Stones. Also in the line-up were The Dave Clark Five, The Hollies, The Swinging Blue Jeans, and The Beatles who were currently Number One. Even faking it, so to speak, Dusty proved herself a cut above the rest. She wore so much mascara that her eyes looked invisible—bringing the quip from Liverpudlian comic Jimmy Tarbuck, 'Dusty Springfield went to London Zoo the other day, and Chi-Chi the panda kept winking at her!' There were more appearances on *Ready, Steady, Go!* and in February she participated in a charity show at the Royal Albert Hall when The Rolling Stones topped the bill. Oddly, Vic Billings was knocked back when he suggested that Dusty appear on *Sunday Night At The London Palladium*—Val Parnell booked The Beverley Sisters instead, and she threw a fit when she watched them audaciously closing the show with 'I Only Want To Be With You'.

In the February, Dusty released her second single, 'Stay Awhile', which peaked at Number 13 in the charts. She had wanted to release a cover of 'Anyone Who Had A Heart', whilst Johhny Franz had been in favour of her recording Gene Pitney's 'Twenty-Four Hours From Tulsa'. Dusty had reservations about the first song: Warwick had performed it so well, she said, far better than herself. Nonsense, of course! She also befriended Warwick—or at least pretended to—when the American singer flew to London to promote 'Walk On By' later in the year. The two would be snapped drinking beer and enjoying a 'chinwag' in an East End pub and shopping in Carnaby Street and Petticoat Lane Market. It was all for show, to keep Burt Bacharach on side in the hope that he would write her the hit song he had promised. Truthfully, Dusty could not stand Warwick, and Warwick would never forgive her, or Cilla Black, for stealing 'Anyone Who Had A Heart'. The fact that both women sang the song far, far better than her was apparently immaterial. 'Tulsa', on the other hand, was she said a great number but would give the fans the wrong impression of her. Would a shy, demure, decent young woman pick up a stranger outside a hotel entrance, as the song suggests, and spend the night with him? It might have been argued that Pitney might not have gone in for casual sex either, if appearances were anything to go by—quite simply because *he* was so neurotic, and gave on the impression that once he got the girl back to his room, he might be too *frightened* to do anything with her!

The new single attracted fewer promotional appearances than its predecessor: therefore Dusty and Vic Billings flew to New York, where the first item on the agenda was a meeting with Burt Bacharach. She had included three of his songs on her debut album, scheduled for a spring release, and Bacharach had kept his promise and written a song especially for her. What this was, she never got around to asking: whilst they were dining in his apartment, Bacharach's secretary kept replenishing the turntable, and one of the songs was Bacharach and David's 'I Just Don't Know What To Do With Myself', the flipside of Tommy Hunt's 1962 hit, 'And I Never Knew'. Dusty was bowled over, and announced that this one would be her next single after 'Stay Awhile'. Before leaving New York, she dropped in at the Mira Sound Studios, where she spent much of the day with Shelby Singleton, with whom she had worked on the Springfields' *Folk Songs From The Hills*. Singleton introduced her to Nashville arranger Jerry Kennedy, and the jamming session which ensued provided her with extra material for her album.

Returning to the UK, Dusty hit the tour trail once more, sharing the bill with Eden Kane. The tabloids went into overdrive. Kane's career was on the slide and it was suggested that Dusty was being paid by his record company to help keep his name in lights until his contract expired. This led to the pair becoming linked romantically, a fabrication which Dusty was happy not to deny because, even this early in her career and despite her intense discretion she was terrified of losing all that she had worked for by being outed. Speculation about her sexuality was temporarily diffused when she told a *Daily Mirror* reporter, 'Yes, I've taken him home to meet my parents.' The fact that Kane (aka Richard Sarstedt) may have been Jewish, and that the O'Brien's were devout Catholics was not mentioned. Neither, apparently, was he her only suitor. If one is to believe the hogwash circulating at the time, Dusty was 'involved' with four other men: one was supposedly The Echoes' Douggie Reece, two others were gay, and the fourth was the happily married (and also Jewish) Burt Bacharach. A fifth contender, Gene Pitney, was added to this list in March when Dusty embarked on a three-week tour of Australasia with him, Gerry & The Pacemakers, and Brian Poole & The Tremeloes. They were all mobbed by 5,000 fans at Sydney Airport, and similar hysteria awaited them in Melbourne, Adelaide and Wellington. In fact, Dusty did not particularly like Pitney, the man who brought on-stage neurasthenia to a whole new level—yet it was he who had the audacity to call *her* a bag of nerves!

From Australia, Dusty flew to Hawaii for a five-day break, her first true holiday in years. Then it was back to Britain, where *A Girl Called Dusty* hit the shops in April 1964 and lost little time getting into the charts, peaking at Number Six and remaining on the bestsellers list for six months. With a denim-clad Dusty on the cover, it contained an excellent cross-section of ballads, R & B, and Motown covers, all of them vastly superior to the originals, and was geared towards the dance-floor Mods with half of the tracks fading accordingly. There is Lesley Gore's 'You Don't Own Me', promoted at the time by Gore as a 'proto-feminist anthem'; Dionne Warwick's 'Wishin' & Hopin''; an upbeat version of Marlene Dietrich's 'Shh, kleines Baby' in which she duets with herself. There is her arrangement of The Supremes' 'When The Lovelight Starts Shining Through His Eyes', and a so-so cover of Lee Dorsey's hammy 'Do Re Mi'. Effortlessly, Dusty makes two Shirelles songs her own: 'Will You Still Love Me Tomorrow?' and 'Mama Said'. Next comes Ray Charles' 'Don't You Know?'—one of the songs The Echoes played for their audition. And finally, the ballads. 'Anyone Who Had A Heart' and 'Twenty-Four Hours From Tulsa' may be the best songs on the album, but John Kander and Fred Ebb's 'My Colouring Book' comes a close third. This had been written for Barbra Streisand in 1962, though Nana Mouskouri had recorded it at the same time and sold more copies.

In May, Dusty flew to Italy, where she spent a week sightseeing in Rome, Naples—and Capri, where she lunched with Gracie Fields at her Canzone del Mare complex and attended a Luigi Tenco concert. Tenco (1939-67) had a deep, smoky voice and sounded a little like Nat King Cole. He specialised in passionate, heartfelt ballads, and Dusty was taken up by his 'Mi sono innamorato di te', which he gave her permission to have adapted into English. Dusty was desperate Cilla Black a run for her money by proving that she did not hold the monopoly on high-powered ballads. Cilla had recently topped the UK charts with 'You're My World', introduced by Tenco's contemporary, Umberto Bindi, another song which Dusty had had her eye on for a while. Now, she called Vic Billings from Rome, told him about the Tenco song, and demanded that 'I Just Don't Know What To Do With Myself' be withdrawn. It was too late in the day to do this, and the record was released without her blessing. It actually sold more copies than 'You're My World'—only The Beatles' 'A Hard Day's Night' and The Rolling Stones' 'It's All Over Now' prevented it from topping the charts. The song was Dusty's best so far, though some critics—and even a few fans—would poke fun at her extraneous gestures while performing it. One wag suggested that the reason she flung her arms up to her face while belting out these powerhouse numbers was because the emotion sometimes got to be too much for her and she forgot the words, therefore she printed these on her wrists! In fact, she was so short-sighted that, even if she had done this, on a darkened stage it would have been impossible to see them. Additionally, the audience would have seen them when the house lights came on. Dusty was not exaggerating when she said that much of the time she could not see the television cameras, even when these were only yards in front of her—a problem which she solved by having the cameraman attach a piece of white card to the tripod. The song, moreso than Cilla's early successes, also set a precedent in that it introduced to Britain a new genre of anguished up-tempo love songs previously championed by Continental stars such as Gribouille ('Mathias') and Francoise Hardy ('All Over The World'). Other British girl singers would attempt this specialised medium: Dusty, Cilla, and Kathy Kirby aside, most of these would prove to be one-hit wonders.

Scarcely pausing to catch her breath, Dusty returned home and hit the tour-circuit, and after spending six weeks zigzagging up and down the country began what should have been a week-long stint in Coventry with The Searchers and Eden Kane. After the fifth show she was forced to bow out, suffering from laryngitis. While she was recovering, Vic Billings was contacted by the organisers of

Murray The K's Extravaganza, a twice-nightly showcase at New York's multiracial 5,000-seater Fox Theater in Brooklyn, after the Apollo in Harlem the most important venue for the city's black community.

Between 1958-9, Murray Kaufman (1922-82) ruled the New York air waves. Single-handedly, he integrated black, white and Latino performers on the same stage long before the US government passed its civil rights laws. More importantly he did so without causing any fuss amongst detractors—once joking that the only ever riots he had incurred had been those en-route to the box-office. Bobby Darin and Dionne Warwick got their big breaks through him, as did Martha Reeves of The Vandellas. Always introduced with a Frank Sinatra song, Kaufman's shows were broadcast from just about anywhere to attract maximum publicity: subways, fighter jets, baseball stadiums—one, in a New York square during a ferocious snowstorm with bikini-clad cheerleaders! A self-confessed megalomaniac and six times married, Kaufman also raised hundreds of thousands of dollars for refugees.

During the early years of Beatlemania, Kaufman was known as The Fifth Beatle—an appellation said to have come from George Harrison. He was the first American DJ accepted into the group's inner circle, after which he developed a mania for absolutely anything Liverpudlian. When his aides had suggested bringing a white singer over from England to perform black songs at the Fox Theater, Kaufman had balked at the idea—his argument being that *only* black singers were capable of singing black music properly. When he heard 'You're My World' on the radio and was erroneously told that this was Liverpool's most famous singer, he changed his mind. It was only when Dusty arrived in New York, with her parents, that Kaufman realised she was not Cilla! His producer wanted to send her packing, but once they had auditioned her in the empty theatre and heard how good she was, they upped her fee for the twenty shows!

Dusty later said that her tenure at the Fox had been like a trip to heaven, for here she was sharing equal billing with names she had only ever dreamed of meeting: Martha & The Vandellas, Marvin Gaye, The Temptations—and The Ronettes, whose dressing room she was asked to share. Also present were Phil and Ronnie Spector, whilst human rights activist Malcom X dropped in each day for a chat. Because of his presence and the tension this caused outside the theatre, once the singers arrived for the morning rehearsal they were not permitted to leave the building until after the show, twelve hours later. Dusty, star-struck from the moment she met these people—though she was as big in her field as they were in theirs, if not bigger—recalled in an interview with Radio One:

> It was a dream come true. It was priceless. I would have *paid* to do it. I was the token whitey, the token honkey....I blundered my way through Harlem not knowing what was around me, a beehive surrounded by pimps, hookers, addicts and pushers. I stayed at the Hotel Teresa, with broken windows. Malcolm X was there. God protects fools and innocents. I grew up fast!

What Dusty did not add was that her first working experience with her R & B idols started off as a nightmare. Upon her arrival in New York there had been no welcoming committee and she had had to make her own way to the theatre, where one of Murray Kaufman's aides had showed her to her dressing room and rudely left her to introduce herself to everyone else. Though she would only be singing two songs in each show ('Wishin' & Hopin'', and 'I Only Want To Be With You'), there would be up to six shows a day, leaving no time for socialising between performances. Kaufman had appointed Martha & The Vandellas as her backing group, and as part of the team effort Dusty would also be expected to back the other singers from the wings.

Meeting Dusty came as a big shock to these people. All of them had heard her on the radio, but few knew what she looked like, and the first thing that hit them was that she was not black. Not that anyone was in any way prejudiced or unfriendly towards her—quite the reverse, they were proud that an attractive white woman had taken it upon herself to champion their style. What they did not anticipate was her unpredictable temper. Her nerves frayed over the fact that she might fail and make a fool of herself, she yelled and cursed whenever she hit a sour note and took a leaf out of her mother's book by flinging whatever crockery was at hand at the walls. Far from criticising her and complaining to the producer, the other artistes simply regarded her as 'the eccentric English girl', and eventually found amusement in her tantrums because they were mostly directed at herself. Martha Reeves would go on to become a close friend—they even put in an impromptu performance at the Apollo, at a time when white artistes just did not appear there—and the other singers adopted Dusty as their lucky mascot on account of her being the only white person on the Fox Theater bill. On a more serious note she began drinking, though not too heavily for now—one of The Temptations is said to have handed her a tumbler of vodka to help calm her nerves, with Dusty apparently so liking the taste that she finished off the bottle.

Immediately after the Kaufman shows, Dusty embarked on what should have been an eight-venue tour of the United

States with Eden Kane and The Searchers. Halfway through this, and thirty minutes before the show in Tulsa, she collapsed from nervous exhaustion—hardly surprising after being cooped in the Fox Theater for ten twelve-hour days without seeing daylight. Neither had she seen much of her parents. Tom had joined them and escorted around New York, and they had flown home without saying goodbye. The doctor who examined her prescribed complete rest, but Dusty insisted on performing: she managed ten songs before leaving the stage. The next day, Vic Billings booked her on a flight to the Caribbean, where she spent ten days relaxing in the sun.

Fully recovered, Dusty returned to England where, on 16 October, her fourth single was released: penned by her brother Tom and Clive Westlake, 'Losing You' (backed with their Top 30 hit for Frank Ifield, 'Summer Is Over') peaked at Number 9 in the charts. Later in the month, she acted as Martha & The Vandella's ambassador when the group arrived in London. She and the trio appeared on *Ready, Steady, Go!* and Dusty took her new friend shopping and sightseeing. Mary Wells had paved the way for Motown artists in Britain by getting 'My Guy' into the Top Five, and soon would be followed across the Atlantic by The Supremes and several other big acts, all of which would be taken under Dusty's wing. There followed a brief tour with Dave Berry, Herman's Hermits, and Brian Poole & The Tremeloes. Each evening, Dusty opened her set with 'Dancing In The Street', and managed to get in two songs that she said she wished she had introduced—Doris Day's 'Secret Love' from *Calamity Jane* (also a recent hit for Kathy Kirby) and Sandie Shaw's 'Always Something There To Remind Me'. She should have appeared in the *Royal Variety Performance* on 8 November, but was replaced at the last minute by Cilla Black which did not bode well with her at all. In early December she released a Christmas single, 'O Holy Child', another song penned by Tom. The record did not chart, though all the royalties went to Dr Bernardo's Homes for disabled children.

In the middle of December, Dusty and her musicians flew to South Africa for what should have been a seven-date tour of the townships surrounding Cape Town, Johannesburg and Port Elizabeth. Hoping to smooth the way in what was expected to be a volatile climate regarding the country's stance on apartheid, Vic Billings had flown on ahead of her. Some years before, George and Beryl Formby had been performing to segregated audiences when a little black girl had walked on to the stage to present them with flowers. Beryl had picked her up, kissed her, and the next day the couple had been asked to leave the country. Instead, they had defied the authorities by performing in the townships to black-only audiences. They had got away with this because according to a loophole in the law, segregation did not apply if the venue was a cinema which seated less than 1,500, though they had eventually been deported. Diana Dors had experienced similar problems during a cabaret tour, and the result had been the same when she had refused to present a sporting award at an event where black sportsmen had been excluded.

Dusty would not prove quite so daring. 'I've got a special clause written into the contract which stipulates that I shall only play to non-segregated audiences. That's my little bit to help coloured people there,' she told the *New Musical Express,* adding that if the South African authorities tried to force her to do otherwise, she would be on the first plane home. Billings had been told that performing to mixed audiences would not be tolerated, but does not appear to have made this clear to Dusty. In his defence, he had booked Dusty *only* in those cinemas where the Formbys and Diana Dors had played, all those years ago. Dusty would be taken to task for not walking off the stage upon seeing the mixed rows of black and white faces. In fact, like George Formby, she was so short-sighted that she could barely see the footlights, let alone who was sitting in the stalls.

When faced with angry officials, Beryl Formby had given as good as she got—telling Daniel Malan, the head of the National Party who introduced apartheid, "Piss off, you horrible little man!" Dusty simply mumbled an apology, and burst into tears. Vic Billings covered his own back by declaring that he had explained the regulations to his client, but that she had refused to listen. The fact that Dusty had already publicly declared she would be donating her entire earnings from this tour—estimated at around £3,000—to orphaned *black* children was also added to her list of 'crimes'. The first two shows in Johannesburg went without hitch—just a handful of racist protesters outside the venue. So too did things appear to be running smoothly during the first shows at the Luxurama Theatre, in Wittebome, an establishment with a no-refunds policy. The authorities had been watching her, however, and on the eve of her fifth of seven concerts she was ordered not to sing in front of a mixed audience—for a non-segregated show which had sold out weeks ago. Not wishing to let these fans down, Dusty did the show. The manager, a Mr. Quibbell, presented her with flowers on the stage, kissed her on both cheeks—then called the military police to complain that she had 'broken the house rules' by boasting of her ability 'to bring blacks and whites together in harmony'. Two hours later, three government officials barged into her hotel suite and served her with a pledge: unless she signed this, swearing not to play before mixed audiences, she would have to leave the country within the next twenty-four hours.

Dusty's refusal to comply resulted in her passport being impounded, and the phone in her room cut off so that she could not make contact with the outside world. She was served with a deportation order and transferred to a hotel in Johannesburg, where she was informed that two seats had been reserved on a flight for London the next day—one for her, the other for Vic Billings. She refused to leave the country without The Echoes: staying in another part of the city. After ploughing through a mountain of red tape, Billings managed to secure everyone seats on the same plane, and early the next evening Dusty and The Echoes were collected from their respective hotels and escorted to the airport by an armed guard. Unable to mingle with the other passengers in the departure lounge they were marched across the tarmac to the waiting plane, where a line of black porters doffed their caps out of respect. Dusty's response, however, to the white official who saluted as she mounted the steps was a pronounced, 'Fuck you!'

The South African government issued a statement: 'Miss Springfield received two warning regarding her flounting of this country's entertainments laws, and twice she refused to comply. She broke the law, and as such has paid the penalty. From today her records will be banned in South Africa.' The British government, recognising this, refused to intervene. At Heathrow, Dusty received a heroine's welcome, cheered by more than a thousand fans. Purposely choosing a black and white chair, she told the barrage of press, 'I may sue the South African government. If they want to sling mud around, they've picked the wrong person because I have a far more deadly aim.' And, she was asked, would she go back if she had the chance? 'Sure,' she replied. 'The audiences were fantastic and the kids were marvellous. But I won't be going back until they sort this thing out, which I don't think will be in my lifetime.'

The debacle continued for several months. Comedian Max Bygraves, one-hit wonders Peter & Gordon, and snooty character actor Derek Nimmo, about to begin working in South Africa, accused Dusty of aggravating the political situation there by organising a publicity stunt and effectively making conditions intolerable there for people like themselves. Dusty responded by calling Nimmo 'a pompous prat'—what she had to say about the others, and most especially Bygraves is best not repeated here.

'I have no political views,' she hit back in an interview which sadly did not receive a wider audience because it was given to *Melody Maker* and not the national press, 'But if anyone pays me the compliment of wanting to watch me on the stage, then they should be allowed to buy a ticket irrespective of colour, creed or religion.'

On the positive side, on 19 December a governmental group headed by fifteen MPs pledged a motion to make a public stand against 'the obnoxious doctrine of apartheid in South Africa'. Shortly after this, the United Nations Special Committee Against Apartheid, aided by singer Miriam Makeba and trumpeter Hugh Masekela, petitioned for an international cultural boycott against South Africa. This helped somewhat—The Searchers, The Zombies, and Eden Kane all cancelled their imminent trips to the country—but as Dusty had predicted, it would take years for this disease to be stamped out altogether.

Four: Don't Let Me Lose This Dream

The New Year dawned with Dusty making a double appearance at the famed San Remo Festival, in Italy. Paired with Fabrizio Ferretti (as per the contest's tradition) she sang 'Tu che ne sai' and was eliminated in the first round. Her second song, 'Di fronte all'amore', which saw her paired with Gianni Mascolo, made it through to the semi-finals—she subsequently recorded this in English as 'I Will Always Want You'. Dusty celebrated her loss by rushing to her room and decimating an expensive vase. The overall winner in 1965 was Bobby Solo & The New Christy Minstrels, with 'Se piang, se ridi'. Dusty thought about having this adapted into English, but instead plumped for the song which came seventh—Pino Donaggio's 'Io che non vivo', of which more later.

In the February, Dusty released Mike Hawker and Ivor Raymonde's 'Your Hurtin' Kinda Love', a dramatic piece which received the thumbs-down from fans, barely scraping into the Top 40. She sang this on *Sunday Night At The London Palladium* before jetting off to New York: 'I Only Want To Be With You' had entered the *Billboard* chart, where it would peak at Number 12. Then it was off to Rio, where she spent five days at the Carnival with Martha Reeves and Madeline Bell, a sojourn which ended when she stepped on a broken bottle, badly gashing her foot. Returning to Britain and in obvious pain, she embarked on the three-week tour with The Searchers. 1964 had seen readers of the *New Musical Express* voting her Top British Female Vocalist, and second only to Brenda Lee in the World category. This led to her performing a set at the magazine's Poll Winners Concert, at Wembley's Empire Pool.

Soon afterwards, Dusty hosted her first television show, a one-hour special entitled *Dusty Springfield Presents The Sound Of Motown*—a title which, prior to its broadcast on 28 April had been whittled down to *The Sound Of Motown*. It coincided with the label's launch in Britain, for which Berry Gordy had assembled a tour with Stevie Wonder, the Supremes, the Miracles, and of course Martha & The Vandellas—the latter's high-charged duet with Dusty of 'Wishin' & Hopin'' was the highlight of the television show. When filming wrapped, a huge Motown party took place in Holland Park where guests of honour were Dusty, The Rolling Stones' Brian Jones, Sandie Shaw, The Seekers and The Animals. The actual tour kicked off on 30 April with a sell-out show at Finsbury Park, though without celebrity support at the subsequent venues they played mostly to 50 per cent capacity audiences. Then for Dusty it was back to the old routine—a Northern clubland tour which coincided with the release of a new single, 'In The Middle Of Nowhere', a rowdy but infectious piece which featured Madeleine Bell and another Springfield regular, ex-gospel singer Doris Troy, on backing vocals, and with the Animal's Alan Price on piano. Unlike its predecessor it had no trouble getting into the Top Ten. Later, Dusty's 'choir' would be augmented by Lesley Duncan and British newcomer Kiki Dee, and under the pseudonym Gladys Thong (to get around the clause in her contract prohibiting her from doing so) Dusty returned the compliment by singing backing vocals on some of their records.

 At around this time, Dusty moved home, renting a flat within a large regency house on Westbourne Terrace, near Hyde Park. The other occupants included Margo Lewis and Carole MacDonald of Goldie & The Gingerbreads, 'Little Arrows' singer Leapy Lee, DJ Stevie Holly, and Madeleine Bell. Vicki Wickham spent so much time here that she later said that she had almost considered herself a resident. Another frequent visitor was Lee Middleton, Billy Fury's partner who later married DJ Kenny Everett. Then there were Dusty's tennis friends, chief of which were Billie Jean King and Rosie Casals. Some of the food-throwing parties here were legendary, especially when the O'Briens came to stay, or if everyone had been smoking pot. Dusty's tenancy here would be brief. Soon afterwards she moved to a three-storey house on Aubrey Walk, which she would share with 'Walking My Cat Named Dog' singer Norma Tanega. The pair had been friends for a while since appearing on television's *Thank Your Lucky Stars*, with the press speculating over whether they were actually lovers. They were, but though Dusty was absolutely terrified of anyone ever finding out, Tanega said she would have loved to have been as outrageous as Madonna, and held nothing back. In those days, of course, homophobia was rife in the music industry and such an admission would not have proved detrimental to their careers.

    Dusty should have played a short summer season in Bournemouth, but this was cancelled when she was admitted to a London clinic suffering from acute nervous exhaustion. Her problem had always been worrying for worrying's sake, searching for problems which were not there, and getting worked up over nothing. Like her idols Peggy Lee and Doris Day, she was a perfectionist: unlike them, she was incapable of handling fame and appears to have been anything but relaxed much of the time, most especially while working in the studio. When it came to musical arrangements, she knew exactly what she wanted and would never settle for second best, flying off the handle with her musicians over the slightest discrepancy. Also, as her career progressed, she became increasingly more paranoid about her appearance. As had happened with some of the stars from the old studio system—Garbo, Dietrich, Crawford—virtually no one was permitted to see her not looking her absolute best. Much as Dusty loved being recognised, despite the frequently flimsy disguise of headscarf and dark glasses, she loathed being photographed unless for an authentic shoot. Like Garbo, if a photographer approached her, she shielded her face with whatever object was closest at hand. Preparation for the performance took longer than the performance itself and invariably involved tremendous personal discomfort. East End drag-queens, who championed Dorothy Squires and Marlene Dietrich, now had a new alter-ego. On planes, so as not to disturb her heavily lacquered wigs, Dusty would sleep for hours sitting bolt upright. The make-up, particularly the mascara, often looked like it had been applied with a trowel to the extent that at times she appeared not to *have* any eyes. Sometimes she would begin fixing this on the plane, not get it finished before the plane landed, and stumble through the airport late at night so that no one would see her 'naked' eyes. She had created this mythical image. Mary O'Brien was dead and buried. The wigs became more elaborate, and were named after rivals—Cilla, Sandie, Lulu, etc. Therefore if one of these singers upset her by 'pinching' one of her songs, or if she was just generally in a bad mood, she could fling the hairpiece across the room or trample it underfoot. The music journalist Keith Altham recalled dropping in at the *Ready, Steady, Go!* studio to find her throwing one of her wigs around: 'I said, "Hi, Dusty. Am I interrupting something?" She said, "I'm just giving Cilla a good kicking!"'

Dusty was paranoid about her off-stage privacy. Friends recall her dashing into the bathroom if room service knocked on the door or if the window cleaner came around. She was also terrified of forgetting the words to her songs, and a bag of nerves before going on stage, convinced that she would mess up and end up with audiences laughing or walking out on her. This never happened. Though she would give the odd mediocre performance towards the end of her life on account of her final illness, the fans always stuck by her and if she did slip up, they prompted her by singing along with the lyrics. Yet if she did make a mistake, Dusty would don the proverbial hair-shirt and feel bad for days. Her only 'cure' came from flinging food at the walls, turning her flat or dressing room into a pig-sty. Then, she would engage in what she called her therapeutic passion—cleaning. Like Joan Crawford, she loved nothing more than getting down on her hands and knees, preferably in an expensive gown, and fettling the place from top to bottom. Shopping was another way of relieving the tension, though as a shopaholic she had been tempered somewhat in the habit by Vic Billings, who at around this time began investing/banking her earnings, said to have been in excess of £2,000 a week, and paying her a weekly allowance.

In September 1965, following an extended holiday in the Virgin Islands, Dusty released a single, 'Some Of Your Lovin'', a heady ballad penned by Gerry Goffin and Carole King which reached Number 8 in the charts. She also released her second album, *Everything's Coming Up Dusty*. Philips spared no expense with the packing: an attractive gatefold sleeve containing a 12-page photo spread mostly of stills from her television appearances, unusual for the time. Technically, this album was better than *A Girl Called Dusty*—there were less fade-outs, for one thing—though despite peaking at Number 6 in the charts it did not sell as many copies, albeit that it has made up for this since.

The album opens well with the gospel-tinged 'Won't Be Long', though with 'Oh No! Not My Baby', a recent hit for Manfred Mann, Dusty is drowned by Madeleine Bell. Next comes Bacharach and David's 'Long After Tonight Is Over', originally a hit for Jimmy Radcliffe, another star who would die tragically young. 'La Bamba' is a traditional song, revived by Richie Havens in 1958 and a hit across the Continent for Dalida. Singing in Spanish here, Dusty is accompanied on the Latin piano by her brother Tom. She does not however fare quite so well with Anthony Newley and Leslie Bricusse's showstopper, 'Who Can I Turn To?', a hit for Tony Bennett which Dionne Warwick had recently murdered. Dusty emulates the Peggy Lee Latin version, which just does not work here. With Ray Charles' 'Doodlin'', something of an upbeat torch song, she fares slightly better. Much better but a little heavy on percussion is 'If It Don't Work Out', written for Dusty by The Zombies' Rod Argent, who provides piano accompaniment. Dusty wanted this to be released as her next single, but Philips overruled her: in the mid-Sixties, unlike today, it was not customary to release singles taken from albums because record companies were afraid that if this happened, fans would only buy one or the other. Above average are 'That's How Heartaches Are Made', and Garnett Mimms' 'It Was Easier To Hurt Him', a recent hit for Wayne Fontana. 'I've Been Wrong Before' is a simplistic reading of the Randy Newman song most associated with Cilla Black. Madeleine Bell and Doris Troy again share the honours with 'I Can't Hear You', 'Packin' Up', and 'I Had A Talk With Your Man'. Dusty had also recorded an excellent version of The Velvettes' 'Needle In A Haystack', but this was dropped when, upon listening to the playback tape, she decided that she no longer liked it.

At the end of October, ignoring her doctor's advice to take things a little easier, Dusty flew to New York, and then to Los Angeles where she spent a week doing the rounds of television variety and chat shows. She was back in London for 14 November, for her only appearance on a *Royal Variety Show*. Topping the bill was Shirley Bassey. Dusty was disappointed that she was asked to sing just one song—'I Just Don't Know What To Do With Myself'—and that more emphasis was placed on her French counterpart, Sylvie Vartan, who with her rocker husband Johnny Hallyday stole the show.

Following an explosive appearance on *Ready, Steady, Go!*'s New Year special which saw a raucous duet with Lulu ('Let's Hang On'), Dusty released her first single of 1966: 'Little By Little' was written for her by 'Middle Of Nowhere' composers Bea Verdi and Buddy Kaye. Another gospel-styled anthem backed by regulars Madeleine Bell, Lesley Duncan and Kiki Dee, it made the Top Twenty, but only after Philips had advertised it in the music press. Dusty admitted to never liking the song which of course begs the question—why record it?

Nothing would ever compare with Dusty's next single. Philips had wanted this to be 'Heartbeat'—not the Buddy Holly hit and later theme of the television drama series, but the Gloria Jones number which the company planned releasing simultaneously in America. Dusty stuck to her guns: she had never been satisfied with their choice of releases there, and from now on declared that nothing would be issued without her approval. Also, though she did not actually dislike Cilla Black, she was irked with the fact that Cilla was selling more records in the UK than herself—for no other reason than Cilla specialised in powerhouse Continental ballads which she seemed to have been born to sing. Dusty therefore decided that her next single on *both* sides of the Atlantic would be an English adaptation of 'Io che non vivo', which Pino Donaggio and his songwriter partner Vito Pallavicini had given her permission to record...on the proviso that their arrangement of the song remain unchanged. Dusty had attempted to write the English lyrics herself, as had Tom, adhering as close as possible to the song's original meaning, 'I can't live without you'. This had not worked and, according to the story, hoping that someone would come up with a solution to her dilemma, Dusty instructed Johnny Franz to book the studio, then asked her friend Vicki Wickham to 'sort it'. Wickham later claimed to have met pop guru Simon Napier Bell that same evening and that between them they had written the lyrics in a matter of hours, which may or may not be true. What *is* important is that they came up with arguably the most important song of Dusty's career.

'You Don't Have To Say You Love Me', recorded (Take 53 of 59) in a stairwell to get the acoustics spot on, is the kind of *symphonie-en-miniature* which would have done a Squires or Garland proud: the stirring horn introduction, the subtle but complicated key-changes, the way the music builds up to a huge crescendo, the intense but simplistic, passionate, heart-on-sleeve lyrics far more sincere than the original Italian ones. Released in March 1966, it shot to the top of the charts giving Dusty her only British Number One, and though it only held the top spot for one week, it provided her flagging confidence with a much needed boost. In America it peaked at Number 4, and proved so popular that the *Everything's Coming Up Dusty* album was retitled to accommodate this as the title-track. Of the many cover versions, arguably the most famous was by Elvis Presley, who recorded it in 1970. With this song, Dusty's very own *hymne a l'amour* which shifted a million copies by the end of the year, she had moved as far from her Motown roots as was possible whilst well aware of the risks she was taking. This was reflected in the mixed public reaction towards it, not helped by her statement that she believed Pino Donaggio's to have been the superior version of the song. Television's *Juke Box Jury* even voted it a 'miss'. Some tabloid journalists wanted to know who the love interest in the song was supposed to be—whether this was a he or a she. In fact, the unnamed recipient of Dusty's affection could just as easily have been her thousands of fans as opposed to one person in particular. At the time of writing, in its many versions Donaggio's song has sold a staggering 80 million records worldwide, but few would argue that it will never really belong to anyone but Dusty Springfield.

In the summer of 1966, Dusty was signed for her first six-part television series, simply titled *Dusty*. The first show aired on 18 August: the 30-piece orchestra was conducted by Johnny Pearson, whilst Madeleine Bell, Lesley Duncan and The Ladybirds provided backing vocals. Her fabulous gowns were created by Rita Reekie and Dusty's couturier friend, Douglas Darnell (who also designed for Diana Dors and Dorothy Squires) in her favourite shades of pink and purple, and frequently complimented by flowers in her hair or pinned to her neckline—not that this mattered much to anyone but her because everything was filmed in monochrome. Dusty wanted these to be short, flouncy dresses for the pop and Motown numbers, ankle-length gowns for the ballads, and refused to compromise. Her 'foible' also applied to the recording studio, even though only the technicians could see her, invariably resulting in her delaying the proceedings in that it took her almost as long to decide on which dress to wear as it did for her to apply her make-up. 'She thought her legs were less than lovely,' *Dusty In Memphis* producer Jerry Wexler recalled. 'And when she finally arrived, she would be swathed in fabric to the floor.'

Petula Clark and Cilla Black incorporated comedy patter into their shows, but with Dusty only the music mattered—

five songs usually, with a guest spot slotted in the middle—and the series presented her with the opportunity to showcase all those songs she had wanted to record, but never got around to. The first show saw her performing material as diverse as the Four Tops' 'Something About You' and the Seekers' 'The Olive Tree' before dueting with the Dudley Moore Trio on 'Dat Dere'. In the second show she sang 'Cockeyed Optimist', raised the roof with the Isley Brothers' 'Take Me In Your Arms', and rounded off the proceedings with 'I Just Don't Know What To Do With Myself'. Show three included 'Twenty-Four Hours From Tulsa' and Paul Francis Webster's 'The Mood I'm In': the special guest was Woody Allen. She opened the fourth jazz-themed show with 'Call Me Irresponsible', dueted with the Four Freshman, and followed this with a stunning interpretation of Doris Day's 'I'll Never Stop Loving You' from the Ruth Etting biopic, *Love Me Or Leave Me*. Her key changes in this difficult song are quite extraordinary. Fans were kept waiting until show five for 'You Don't Have To Say You Love Me'. In the final show she sang Mary Wells' 'You Lost The Sweetest Boy'—and 'Anna', in 'cod' Spanish, accompanying herself on the guitar and emulating the way Peggy Lee had performed songs such as 'Manana'. Finally there was the Sammy Cahn standard, 'To Love And Be Loved'.

'You Don't Have To Say You Love Me' was still in the lower reaches of the charts when the series aired, and its successor, Gerry Goffin and Carole King's 'Goin' Back' had just entered the Top Ten. With its plaintive piano introduction and powerfully undulating strings, the lyrics of this wistful pastiche are deceptively simple but emotive, expressing the narrator's yearning to return to those innocent childhood days the singer claimed to have loved so much. To add to the ambiance, Dusty took her mascot, a moth-eaten teddy bear named Einstein, into the booth when she recorded it. There had been competition in the form of an inferior version by Dusty's friends, Goldie & The Gingerbreads, but their single had been forcibly withdrawn after they had changed the lyrics without acquiring the composers' permission. Two years later, The Byrds would include it on their *Notorious Byrd Brothers* album, and many years later there would be a tremendous version by Marianne Faithfull. Equally stirring was its successor, 'All I See Is You', Clive Westlake's torchy ballad which Dusty released in the September. This reached Number 9 in the UK, Number 20 in America. Philips also put out her first compilation album, *Golden Hits*, which narrowly missed hitting the top spot and stayed in the charts for nine months.

In October, Dusty hit the road, headlining above The Alan Price Set and Dave Berry. *Melody Maker* and the *New Musical Express* voted her Top British Female Singer, but whilst she was making headlines in the music press, she also provided fodder for the tabloids. The first was related to her obsession with throwing things. One evening, in a London restaurant, she threw the first thing that came to hand—a meat pie—at a waiter who she thought was being rude to a young female customer. A perfect aim, this hit him across the back of the head. Her 'reprehensible' behaviour—compared to the antics of some of today's stars, very tame—was recounted on several front pages, but it was Dusty who had the last word. 'I would never dream of throwing a common meat pie at anyone,' she told one hack, 'It was a *quiche-lorraine*—much more up-market!'

Another more serious incident resulted in a dangerous driving charge. Driving late at night in her sports car and wearing sunglasses to disguise her unmade-up eyes, Dusty hit an old lady crossing Berkeley Square. She was so hysterical after the accident that the paramedics took her to the hospital with the patient. Both she and her unnamed female passenger admitted to the police that it had been her fault entirely, and the matter was turned over to the courts. Unfortunately, the hearing slipped Dusty's mind and when the case was heard at the end of the month she had left England for New York to play a three-week season at Basin Street East. As soon as she realised her gaff, she wired a cheque to the old lady as a down-payment for the damages she knew she would have to pay. In her absence, the judge found her guilty, and awarded the victim £2,000 in damages.

Dusty would not forget Basin Street East in a hurry. The swanky nightclub inside the Sheldon Towers Hotel (now the Shelton Grill) had played host to some of the biggest names in jazz-contemporary music: Peggy Lee had famously played here in 1961. Dusty had been booked for two shows a night, three on weekends, which meant that she would be singing upwards of thirty songs with not much of a break between performances. The supporting act was Buddy Rich (1917-87), the self-proclaimed 'world's greatest drummer', and arguably one of the most odious men in American show business. Even his entourage secretly filmed his tantrums and vulgar outbursts and played them back to him, to no avail, in the hope of getting him to clean up his act. In the near future, Rich almost make a second career out of his hatred of the Osmonds, telling one British chat show host in a live programme that his greatest ambition was to 'stamp on Little Jimmy Osmond's head'. Rich also hated female entertainers, most especially if they were not American, and at Basin Street East aimed his vitriol at Dusty *before* she arrived at the venue, getting his aides to change the sign above the entrance so that his name appeared above hers, and in bigger letters.

Rather than complain, Dusty tried to suck up to Rich's non-existent better nature—suggesting a jamming session in the hope that he and his musicians might join her on stage for a couple of numbers. Rich's response, repeated by a blushing Dusty in a *Q* magazine interview shortly after his death, was a spat out, 'You fucking broad. Who do you think you fucking are, bitch?' Peggy Lee had faced a similar barrage of insults, and simply walked away. Dorothy Squires had *thought* about 'belting him one'. Dusty went the whole hog and rewarded him with a resounding crack across the face, and as she moved away one of her rings caught in his toupee, whipping this off his head and bringing guffaws of laughter from others in the room at the time. 'What a bastard,' she told *Q*, 'He was the arsehole of the world.' Rich threatened to sue her for assault, but opted not to do so when she called his bluff and told him to go ahead—there were plenty of witnesses to the incident, and what he had said. Instead, he took to insulting her on stage in front of the audience, who initially believed it to be but part of a comedy repartee, until made wiser by the press. Rich would introduce her with, 'She's supposed to be a great singer, but I've heard better.'—or, 'She'll be singing "Sunny", so let's hope that it rains on the broad.' His vilest put down was when he said of her, 'She's third-rate, just like all those black broads she favours.' And Dusty would walk meekly on to the stage and give him two fingers. Some nights, Rich's cronies would come to Basin Street East and encourage him in his despicable behaviour, though Dusty emerged from the situation smelling of roses when other stars turned up to support her. One was bandleader Benny Goodman, another Peggy Lee—the only time they ever met—who congratulated her on her choice of material. Peggy later said that Dusty's interpretation of Billie Holiday's 'God Bless The Child' had made her cry.

Dusty's feud with Rich also ensured that she sang to a packed house every performance. At the end of the run, Rich's musicians—who allegedly only stayed with him because he paid them so well, came back on stage and presented her with a pair of boxing gloves. Attached was the message, 'To our champ. You were brave enough to do what we couldn't.'

Towards the end of the year, Dusty found herself signing up for the time-honoured British tradition of pantomime. She had known the country's top drag artiste, Danny La Rue, for a while. His specialities during the mid-Sixties included celebrity gay icons Marlene Dietrich, Dorothy Squires, Carol Channing—and Dusty, who had attended his long-running camp spectacular, *Queen Passionella & The Sleeping Beauty*, the previous year. Meeting producer Tom Arnold after the show, Dusty had joked that it had always been a dream of hers to play pantomime, and in October Arnold called her in New York. He and Bernard Delfont wanted her for *Merry King Cole* at the Liverpool Empire. At first she said no, having just turned down *Dick Whittington* opposite Eden Kane at the Westcliff Pavillion. Delfont made her an offer she could not refuse—£2,000 a week, and full control over her choice of songs for the show. Dusty still hedged, claiming that her fans would never accept her as principal boy—she did not wish to wear a skimpy costume and show her legs but more crucially she was more worried about the press speculating over her sexuality, should she play a man. Delfont informed her that she would be permitted to wear whatever she wanted, and that her part in the show would be a 'mini-recital' towards the end. Furthermore, she would not have to interact with the rest of the cast if she did not want to. Tremulously, she signed the contract and commissioned six floor-length gowns from Douglas Darnell.

Merry King Cole opened to rave reviews on 9 January 1967. Dusty got along well with her co-stars—Blackpool Circus clown Charlie Cairoli, comic Peter Goodwight, and singing twins Paul & Barry Ryan—but still took Delfont up on his offer to bill her as 'a show within a show'. She sang six songs, including both sides of her soon to be released single, 'I'll Try Anything'—this one reached Number 13. The B-side, 'The Corrupt Ones', an odd choice for a pantomime, was sung by Dusty over the credits of a German espionage film, *Die Holle von Macao*, starring Robert Stack and Elke Sommer. After performing this, she led the audience into a sing-along—adopting the snooty mien of an old-fashioned schoolma'am, she stood in front of a large screen and used a large screen to point out the words to Chris Montez's 'The More I See You' and the Beatles' 'Yellow Submarine'. Each performance saw her finishing to a standing ovation, but when the run ended she made it clear that her first pantomime season would also be her last.

On 8 May, Dusty opened at London's Talk of the Town, the city's premiere cabaret establishment situated at the corner of Charing Cross Road and Leicester Square. Formerly the Hippodrome (to which it would revert in 1982 when purchased by Peter Stringfellow), the venue would host legendary appearances by some of the world's greatest gay icons, including Judy Garland and Eartha Kitt. She was booked here for three weeks, longer than the usual season, for a fee of £3,000 a week, putting her in the same salary bracket as Shirley Bassey, who attended the first night. She was accompanied by the club's resident orchestra, directed by Bert Rhodes, who suggested that she slightly amend her Motown-inspired repertoire to fit in with the posh dining crowd's more sophisticated tastes. For Dusty, this posed no problem: her only condition was that she should be allowed to use her own backing singers, headed by Madeleine Bell.

She opened with Dorothy Squires' (then) opener, 'I Only Want To Laugh'—she too was in the audience, and led the standing ovation—and closed with Dalida's arrangement of 'La Bamba'. In between, the highlights of the evening were 'My Colouring Book', a new Italian song called 'Give Me Time', Burt Bacharach's 'The Look Of Love', and of course 'You Don't Have To Say You Love Me'. The showstoppers on most nights were Charles Aznavour's 'Yesterday When I Was Young', Luigi Tenco's 'Senza parole' (which she never recorded) and Jacques Brel's signature tune, 'Ne me quitte pas', which she partly sang in flawless French, sending shivers down the spine. 'The song is about fear and rejection,' she told *Woman* magazine a few years later. 'It's that first day at school feeling. Don't go away and leave me, Mama. It's the kind of feeling that can stay with you through life and become obsessive.' As had happened at Beal Street East, it was standing room only every evening.

The Talk of the Town audiences may have loved Dusty's sweeping, highly emotive Continental ballads but there was no pleasing some fans who, having been fed a giddy diet of Motown, were unprepared for such overt sophistication. Even those who had rushed out in droves to buy 'You Don't Have To Say You Love Me' and 'Goin' Back' appeared to give a thumbs-down to Pietro Melfa's otherwise excellent 'Give Me Time', when this was released as a single to coincide with Dusty's London triumph. Neither did DJs on both sides of the Atlantic help by persistently playing the B-side, 'The Look Of Love', as a result of which the record stalled at Number 24 in the British charts, and at 22 in America. And yet, later on when her career was floundering, she confessed to disliking this type of venue, particularly in America, telling Jean Rook, 'I hate the grey world of night clubs, stuffed with people eating and drinking—who hadn't come to see Dusty Springfield, but who'd just wondered, "Say, Myron, who's on in the Blue Room tonight?"'

By early June, Dusty was back in the studio filming her second television series, to be broadcast in the autumn. The format was the same as before: six 30-minute shows produced by Stanley Dorman, with the emphasis this time placed on the sort of material she had performed in cabaret. Interspersed with the rowdy Motown classics and Italian standards were Hollywood show tunes: 'My Foolish Heart', 'Pick Yourself Up', 'Let's Get Away From It All', 'Do-Re-Mi', 'If My Friends Could See Me Now', and Judy Garland's 'By Myself'. And if she had suffered one braggart across the waves—Buddy Rich—she encountered another on home ground when 'Velvet Fog' crooner Mel Torme guested, and insisted on singing three songs instead of the customary one. Tom Jones, Engelbert Humperdinck and José Feliciano, on the other hand, she loved working with, though her favourite guest was Scott Walker, who sang a selection of Jacques Brel classics.

The television shows in the can, Dusty and Norma Tanega flew to Australia where she played a three-week season at Chequers, in Sidney, a venue whose owners were renowned for getting exactly who they wanted on account of the astronomical fees they offered—in Dusty's case, £5,000 a week. Australian Equity rules dictated she would have to use in-house musicians, but when she arrived there was no bass player, so she paid The Echoes' Douggie Reece to fly out and join her. She was also assigned a personal hairdresser, celebrity stylist John Adams, who persuaded her to ditch her wigs, on account of the heat, and let him work his magic on her locks. Rosemary Clooney was in town, and was so enamoured of Adams' talent that she told friends she was thinking of inviting him to America to work exclusively for her. Dusty got there first. On her last night at Chequers, she gave Adams an envelope containing a first-class air ticket to London and promised to help him set up a salon there. Clooney half-jokingly threatened to tear her hair out by the roots! Soon afterwards, Adams moved to Carnaby Street.

From Sydney, Dusty flew to New York to promote her latest American single, 'What's It Gonna Be?' Then it was off to Bermuda for a series of cabaret engagements. By now, she was introducing 'tribute medleys' into her shows: some evenings she would sing a fifteen-minute Aretha Franklin or Dionne Warwick selection, or if the evening called for a mellow, more relaxed setting she would pay homage to the *chanson*, or Peggy Lee—Dusty's readings of Charles Trenet's 'I Wish You Love' and Peggy's 'Mr Wonderful' were nothing short of amazing. She introduced a comedy sketch which was high-camp at its most profound: wearing ringlets, short polka-dot dress and pumps, she was joined on stage by four mincing sailors and mimicked Shirley Temple—singing 'Animal Crackers In My Soup' and 'The Good Ship Lollipop' in a high-pitched voice in front of a screen where the real child star was performing these with the sound dubbed.

Dusty was in Bermuda when she learned that the new single had only just made the Top 40. It mattered little to her that there had been standing room only at her shows. She, who loved meeting people, would spend hours in her dressing room with adoring fans after a show—then go home and sink into the blackest depression, fretting over record sales. To her way of thinking she had suffered a flop on the eve of Philips releasing her third studio album, and she now was convinced now that this would bomb because the jazz-show tunes-soul-*chanson* material did not befit the 'pop art' cover. This depicted her in monochrome, wearing a picture hat and mini skirt, standing knock-kneed and with an orange psychedelic bubble coming out of her mouth—asking by way of the album's title, *'Where Am I Going?'* 'My last single was a dud,' she told journalists. 'And when the critics see this cover they'll think I'm taking the piss.' It *was* a silly cover, albeit in keeping with the Flower Power times, but her request to have it changed was denied. Effectively, she was worrying over nothing. At the time of its release the album may have sold less copies than its predecessors, but contents and quality-wise it was better than all of them.

Where Am I Going? opens with Cissy Houston's 'Bring Him Back', part-penned by Mort Shuman, who besides being responsible for some of Elvis Presley's biggest hits shared honours with Rod McKuen of adapting and introducing the works of Jacques Brel to the English speaking world—McKuen's adaptation of 'Ne me quitte pas', with which Dusty is almost unrivalled save of course by Brel himself, is also here. 'Don't Let Me Lose This Dream' and 'I Can't Wait to See My Baby's Face' were Dusty's tribute to Aretha Franklin, though whereas Franklin tends to squawk them, Dusty makes a concerted effort to sing them properly. Next there are Evie Sands' 'Take Me For A Little While', Betty Everett's 'Chained To A Memory', and Bobby Hebb's 'Sunny' which Dusty had performed at Basin Street East. Upon hearing that Dionne Warwick had complained about her purloining her songs, Dusty 'nicked' another one—Bacharach and David's 'They Long To Be Close To You', long before The Carpenters made it their own. After Chip Taylor's 'Welcome Home' (not to be confused with the later Peters & Lee song of the same name) we have Alan Jay Lerner's 'Come Back To Me', which Yves Montand sings to Barbra Streisand in *On*

A Clear Day You Can See Forever. 'Broken Blossoms' is a traditional anti-war song rearranged by her brother Tom. And finally there is the title-track, which Dorothy Fields and Cy Coleman had written for Juliet Prowse to sing in *Sweet Charity*. Like 'My Way', this is a 'trooper' anthem associated with someone much older than twenty-eight: the lonely woman, alone on the shelf, her own worst enemy because she has screwed up every relationship so far and now finds herself atoning for her folly because, 'No matter where I go, I meet myself there.'

1968 was a year of ups and downs, triumphs, tantrums and cancellations. Dusty spent much of it zipping back and forth across the Atlantic, fulfilling club and cabaret engagements, and always seeming to be in the wrong place at the wrong time where promotions were concerned. She should have performed Bacharach and David's 'The Look Of Love' at the Academy Awards—the song, which she sang over the soundtrack of the spoof Bond film, *Casino Royale*, had been nominated for an Oscar, but at the last minute she backed out, declaring that she was far too busy to take up a whole evening singing just one song. A few years later she dueted on it with Mireille Mathieu, she singing in English, Mireille in French. In Amsterdam, on 6 March, she ran foul of the promoters of the prestigious *Grand Gala du Disque* by acting the prima donna and making extraneous demands. Firstly she complained about the lack of rehearsal facilities. Next she demanded that more attention be afforded her than fellow contributor Vikki Carr, declaring that Carr had spent less time in the charts than she had, and therefore was of less importance. Her outburst, peppered with expletives, was caught on camera and she was given her marching orders. Dusty unfairly blamed the fiasco on Vic Billings for booking her at the event in the first place, and came close to firing him.

More fireworks were expected later in the month when Dusty appeared on *Sunday Night At The London Palladium*—Buddy Rich was on the bill. The drummer sent a message to her dressing room saying that he wanted to bury the hatchet. Dusty's response was that so did she—in the top of his head! Their respective managers thankfully kept them apart. Rich was even pencilled in as a guest for her third television series, until the producer realised that this might not be such a good idea. Entitled *It Must Be Dusty*, this one was aired on ATV and was a distinct comedown from its predecessors—badly produced and staged, with too much emphasis on the black music as opposed to the more sophisticated material with which she had been wowing cabaret audiences. Additionally, she had no say in the guest list—mostly B-listers, the exceptions being Scott Walker, Georgie Fame, and Julie Felix. A big scoop was wild man Jimi Hendrix, who against everyone's expectations and belief dueted with her on 'Mockingbird', at one point plucking the guitar with his teeth. This performance aside, the critics were mostly disapproving, and as had happened with the Amsterdam fiasco, Vic Billings found himself taking the rap. This time Dusty did fire him—though so far as the press were told, the parting of the ways was amicable. Billings retaliated by serving her with a writ for £30,000 in estimated future commission earnings, but the matter was settled out of court when Dusty paid him £20,000. One of Billings' final jobs had been securing her £10,000 for her most unusual engagement so far—plugging Mother's Pride bread! In the 30-seconds commercial a tomboyish, wigless Dusty is seen pushing her cart along a narrow provincial street, singing 'I'm a happy knocker-upper' while delivering loaves on the end of poles to the customer's bedroom windows!

In the June, Dusty released Clive Westlake's sublime 'I

Close My Eyes And Count To Ten', almost a *chanson* in that it was three melodies rolled into one, and one which Vic Billings had earmarked for Kiki Dee. After her recent small crop of failures she expected this one to bomb too, but it proved a deserved hit and a showpiece for future live appearances, reaching Number 5 in the charts. Its success coincided with Dusty signing a US contract with Atlantic Records, the idea being that she would record equally in Britain and America, with each company releasing the other's records. Initially, there would be three albums. In the September, as part of the Atlantic deal—accompanied by hairdresser John Adams—Dusty flew to Memphis to work on her first album. Her self-esteem was at an all-time low, convinced as she was that her career was spinning out of control and veering towards disaster. It was time, she said, to sink or swim, to search for new horizons. She told the columnist Jean Rook:

> I was seduced by the Great American Dream. I thought it would rekindle the challenge I'd lost here, and initially it did—until I got mixed up with their great record company conglomerates. You begin to feel like a tax write-off to the accountants you never even see—and in the awful sort of greed that settled in in the Seventies.

Dusty's fragile psyche cannot have been helped when she saw the American Studios, a cluster of dilapidated buildings next to the Hertz Village black ghetto. The place had not seen a lick of paint in years, and was plagued with rats. But, she was told, if this had been good enough for Aretha Franklin, who was she to argue?

Dusty had performed unadulterated soul before, but had never recorded a full album of the genre. And who better to produce than the legendary Jerry Wexler? Atlantic Studios had been founded in 1947 by Herb Abramson and Ahmet Ertegun. During the next decade their big stars had been The Drifters. Wexler (1917-2008), accredited with coining the phrase rhythm and blues, had produced such greats as Ray Charles and Bob Dylan. Dusty, he declared, belonged in the 'blue-eyed soul' category currently occupied by Sonny and Cher. He brought in ace engineer Tom Dowd, and assembled a fine group of musicians: The Memphis Cats comprised pianist Bobby Woods, guitarist Reggie Young, and bassist Tommy Cogbill—previously they had backed Elvis Presley and Wilson Pickett. Dusty initially disapproved of Cogbill, for no other reason than she had wanted John Paul Jones, who had accompanied her at the Talk of the Town. Jones, who could play just about every musical instrument known to man, was indisposed, having recently formed Led Zeppelin. It was Dusty who personally met with the Atlantic executives to plead with them, to make up with 'foisting' Cogbill onto her, to at least offer the band a contract. They did, to the tune of $200,000, then a record fee for signing for a new outfit.

As had happened when the Springfields had recorded in America, Dusty had no say in her choice of material. Earlier in the year, at his Long Island home, Wexler had presented her with eighty songs and, not surprisingly for a perfectionist who prided herself in her eclectic repertoire, she had dismissed every single one. 'Although she was ravishingly gorgeous, her doubts and insecurities had amounted to neurosis,' Wexler recalled, well aware that any neurosis had been inflicted by himself by trying to force her to do something against her will. What he did not also add was how rudely he behaved towards her, of how this had led to innumerable in-studio rows which had culminated with her flinging a heavy glass ashtray at him.

Now, eighty songs were whittled down to twenty, and still she was dissatisfied. Neither did Wexler and his team help by persistently singing the praises of their golden girl, Aretha Franklin, leaving Dusty plagued with doubts that she would never be fit to follow in her footsteps—quite the opposite, for she ran rings around the over-loud, screeching American singer. 'Why are you bothering to record me when you can't stop talking about *her*?' she complained at the time. Feeling bullied, she supervised the orchestrations and the backing from the Sweet Temptations (one of these was Cissy Houston, the mother of Whitney), but refused to sing a note until Wexler had found her a studio away from 'Arethaland'—resulting in the album's title, *Dusty In Memphis* becoming something of a misnomer. 'All hell ensued,' Wexler recalled. 'The psychic struggle between Dusty and me was Machiavellian.'

Some years later, Dusty defended herself against this at times obnoxious man. 'What he didn't realise was how intimidated I was,' she told BBC Radio One's *The Atlantic Story*. 'If there's one thing that intimidates good singing, it's fear—allowing the natural critic within me to criticize a note *before* it even left my throat, which destroys the flow of anything!' Yet, though she had few good things to say about him over the coming months, it was Wexler who baptised her 'The Great White Lady'. 'Dusty had the stigmata of perfectibility,' he recalled of the New York sessions in the BBC documentary, *Definitely Dusty*, 'When she [finally] did perform she was afraid to let it go because her standards were so high, and it might not come out exactly right.'

With Wexler still at the helm, but with a minimum of personnel, the recording of the album was transferred to a New York studio. Because it had been drilled into her that she would never be in the same 'league' as Aretha Franklin

Dusty went through a brief period hating the sound of her own voice—asking Wexler for so much track while laying down her vocals that, absolutely deafened by what came through the headphones she was *unable* to hear herself. She also caused the producer grief by insisting upon working in the early hours of the morning, at a time he felt he should have been at home in bed.

Whilst she was recording in America, Philips released her fourth studio album for them, *Dusty...Definitely*, co-produced by herself and Johnny Franz. Much in the vein of *Where Am I Going?* this was promoted as having a 'black' side—the upbeat, Motown-style material—and a 'white' side representing her cabaret work. Atlantic did not consider this sufficiently commercial for the kind of artiste they represented—Wexler was against Philips' policy of allowing her to choose her own songs—therefore they backed out on their deal to release it Stateside. Dusty ranted and raved. What did *they* know about talent? Very little, it would appear if they were foolish enough to reject this one, an excellent album, classy, way ahead of its time. It may have only reached Number 30 in the UK charts, but sales have more than made up for this since. Like the great song stylists she revered—Peggy Lee, Tony Bennett, Nat King Cole—not getting into the charts did not necessarily mean that their albums did not outsell the ones which did, in the long run.

Dusty...Definitely opens with the Temptations' 'Ain't No Sun Since You've Been Gone' which she follows with Erma (sister of Aretha) Franklin's 'Take Another Little Piece Of My Heart'—also covered by Janis Joplin. Bacharach and David's 'Another Night' is next, a hit for Timi Yuro. Next up is Jerry Butler's 'Mr Dream Merchant', and Diana Ross's 'I Can't Give Back The Love I Feel For You'. Closing Side One is Teddy Van's 'Love Power'. Side

Two opens with Bacharach and David's 'This Girl's In Love With You', a hit for German actress-singer Hildegard Knef, though it was Herb Alpert who took the male version to the top of the American charts. Knef had also had a hit with 'No Sad Songs For Me', a phrase which Dusty incorporates into Dorothy Squires' 'I Only Want To Laugh', an optimistic piece which precedes her definitive interpretation of Charles Aznavour's 'Qui', adapted into English as 'Who Will Take My Place?'—his 'Yesterday When I Was Young' and 'La bohéme' were already in her cabaret repertoire. Next, her tribute to Peggy Lee with a stunning rendition of Randy Newman's torchy ballad, 'I Think It's Gonna Rain Today'. Peggy had included this on her forthcoming album, *A Natural Woman*, which caused a bust-up between Dusty and Jerry Wexler, who had co-written the title-track with Gerry Goffin and Carole King for Aretha Franklin to record the previous year. Dusty got hold of the master tape, and told Wexler that, in her opinion, Peggy Lee could *snore* better than Franklin would ever be able to sing! After Gilberto Gil's so-so 'Morning', the proceedings round off with Sammy Cahn and Jimmy Van Heusen's 'Second Time Around', which Frank Sinatra confessed had made him weep. All of her moods are represented on this album, yet just as we are regaining our breath after this last item, Dusty surprises us. The engineer had left the tape running when someone had wheeled the refreshments trolley into the studio, and she was seething from the latest row with Wexler—and now we hear an almighty crash as she hurls its contents to against the wall!

This 'dodgy' year ended on a positive note when Philips released John Hurley and Ronnie Wilkins' slightly risqué 'Son-Of-A-Preacher-Man', from the forthcoming *Dusty In Memphis* album. Just as she had triumphed with songs purloined from Dionne Warwick, so Dusty got one over on

Aretha Franklin by getting a song she had rejected into the Top Ten on both sides of the Atlantic—delighted that Jerry Wexler's persistent boasting about his star protégé had backfired on him. Somehow, the tale of the eponymous Billy-Ray who falls for the girl who finds it hard to be good should have been more suited to Baptist minister's daughter Franklin, who did eventually record it. Dusty, the otherwise 'shy Catholic girl', gives a better delivery because she does so tongue-in-cheek and with restraint.

Dusty In Memphis was released with a fanfare of publicity in April 1969, with fans and critics hailing it one of her best. *Rolling Stone* could not praise it enough: 'Most white female singers in today's music are still searching for music they can call their own. Dusty is not searching—she just shows up and she, and we, are better for it.' Four decades later the magazine would still be applauding her 'blazing soul and sexual honesty that transcended both race and geography', voting it Number 89 in their *500 Greatest Albums Of All Time* poll. Yet at the time it amounted to no more than a Pyrrhic victory for Dusty, selling considerably less copies than her previous albums—100,000 in America before being deleted—and failing to chart on both sides of the Atlantic. Rather than lift her spirits it left Dusty feeling more despondent than ever. The reason for its comparative failure had less to do with the album's content—her choice of material was first-class, as were the performances and arrangements—than her reluctance to adequately promote it. Also, like many middle-of-the-road artistes who had risen to prominence in the early Sixties, a shift in musical trends had forced her career into an undeserved hiatus.

The album starts off with Cynthia Weill and Barry Mann's 'Just A Little Lovin'', an optimistic, feel-good piece later covered by the songwriting duo's greatest champion, Barbra Streisand. Making love early in the morning, Dusty coquettishly proclaims, gives her a bigger buzz than coffee, and sets her in good stead for the rest of the day. If only everyone adopted the practice, she concludes, what a better world this would be! Next, the first of four Goffin-King songs, 'So Much Love', which they had written for Ben E King. After 'Son-Of-A-Preacher-Man' is Randy Newman's 'I Don't Want To Hear It Any More', the tale of the girl from the poor neighbourhood where everyone knows everyone's business, where gossip ruins clandestine love affairs. In Goffin and King's 'Don't Forget About Me', Dusty sets her lover free in the hope that she will be fondly remembered, should their paths cross again. Eddie Hinton's 'Breakfast In Bed' sees Dusty at her most sensual, and executes a neat spin on her biggest hit as she champions straightforward sex without its amorous complications: 'Breakfast in bed and a kiss or three....you don't have to say you love me!' In gay clubs, this would be much favoured by her Sapphic sisters, and later the song would be less endearingly reprised by UB40 featuring Pretenders' singer Chrissie Hynde. 'Just One Smile' returns Dusty to the pen of Randy Newman, and the number she shared with Gene Pitney. Nobody cares if she cries, so she will pretend that her lover is still here, though in the end she throws in the towel and concludes, 'It's so hard to forget when your whole world you know is dying!'

Dusty had sung Brel, Aznavour, Charles Trenet (I Wish You Love), and Piaf just the once—'When The World Was Young'. Now she turned to Michel Legrand's 'Les moulins de mon coeur', adapted into English by two more Streisand stalwarts, Alan and Marilyn Bergman. Noel Harrison had introduced the song over the soundtrack of *The Thomas Crown Affair*, but not nearly so well as this. Dusty's reading strongly adheres closely to the version recorded by French chanteuse Frida Boccara: breathy, emotive, and convincing as she uses poetic, psychedelic imagery to describe her inner turmoil following the break-up of yet another relationship. Life does not get much brighter in Burt Bacharach's 'In The Land Of Make Believe', the weakest song on the album which sees Dusty emulating Blossom Dearie and straining in an uncustomary squeaky voice: the lover is far away, perhaps gone for good, but she can still pretend that he/she is still here and that they are kissing in their long-dead paradise—for as long as she keeps up the pretence, they will always be together. As with *Where Am I Going?* the album closes on a self-pitying note. Goffin and King's 'No Easy Way Down' is a 'can't-do-right-for-doing-wrong' pastiche—the fact that one might *think* one has attained the giddy heights of love, in the real world there is no such thing as that crock of gold at the rainbow's end, just one more disappointment such as the one in 'I Can't Make It Alone', Goffin and King's final contribution to the album. Here, Dusty begs the lover she hurt to forgive her and reach out to save her dying soul—for no other reason than she can no longer cope with the pain of loneliness.

For Dusty, things appeared to be going from bad to worse. 1969 was promised to be her busiest year ever—a predicted non-stop round of tours and recording sessions. The comparative failure of *Dusty In Memphis* put paid to this. During the spring she toured North America and Canada, promoting 'Windmills Of Your Mind'. The single just scraped into the *Billboard* Top 40, and though the first few dates sold out fairly quickly, attendances for the rest of the tour were poor—less than 50 per cent in some venues. An autumn tour of the campuses was cancelled, along with a cabaret season at New York's Americana Club. Dusty also lost her favourite backing singer. Madeleine Bell, a fine artiste in her own right, joined singer-songwriter Roger Cook, Alan Parker, and Herbie Flowers to found the group,

Blue Mink: starting with their racial harmony anthem, 'Melting Pot', they would enjoy seven UK Top 30 hits over the next four years. Disgruntled—there would be little contact between them from now on—Dusty returned to London where, pleased to be going back to the BBC, she taped her next eight-part television series, *Decidedly Dusty*, to begin broadcasting in the September.

This series was a distinct improvement on the last. Back to being allowed to select her own guests, she opted for Jimmy Ruffin and her favourite comedienne, Lamb Chop ventriloquist Shari Lewis. Her special guest in one show was Danny La Rue, who impersonated her singing 'I Just Don't Know What To Do With Myself'. For the final show, the producers had wanted Lulu, the joint winner (with France's Frida Boccara, the Netherlands' Lenny Kuhr, and Spain's Salomé) of the *Eurovision Song Contest* that year. Dusty requested Boccara (1940-96), a truly magnificent chanteuse who died tragically young, and who brought the house down with the English version of 'Un jour, un enfant'. A few years later, when preparing a television spectacular with Juliet Prowse and Burt Bacharach, Dusty would ask for Boccara but instead be given Mireille Mathieu. The trio would deliver an electrifying ten-minute tribute to The Beatles. To coincide with the series, Philips released 'Am I The Same Girl?' which peaked at a disappointing Number 43 in the charts. Dusty blamed the record company for bringing it out at the wrong time, though there was hardly a right time—when not filming television specials in Europe, she was zipping back and forth across the Atlantic to work on her next album.

In November 1969, Atlantic put out 'A Brand New Me', a track off *From Dusty...With Love*, the last time her name would be used in a contemporary album title. Some years later, this would appear in the *Guardian*'s *1,000 Albums To*

Hear Before Yor Die list. The single reached Number 25 in the US charts, prompting Atlantic to change the album's title to *A Brand New Me*. Dusty threw a fit and dropped the song from her repertoire. Next, in an expletives charged tirade, she turned on Jerry Wexler when he suggested another recording session in Memphis: she would not, she declared, be working again here—or in New York, *or* with any of the musicians from the *Dusty In Memphis* sessions. She also flatly refused to have anything to do with pianist Bobby Woods, who she accused of homophobia. Some years later, speaking to biographer Lucy O'Brien, Woods confessed that he had had reservations about her 'sexual reputation'. 'It was a kinda icky situation,' he said, 'I didn't want to get too close to it....In the country where I came from, if someone found out someone was homosexual you either got hung or run out of town. Eight years on, in Los Angeles, echoing similar comments made by Elizabeth Taylor, Dusty told a reporter from *Gay News:*

> There's a very strong anti-gay feeling here, which is extraordinary in an industry which is 75 per cent gay. Because industry heads are very anti-gay it's very tough for most gay people and difficult to speak out....I respect gay people. That doesn't make me one, and that doesn't *not* make me one. But I have a gay following and I'm grateful for it.

Little wonder then, when faced with such hypocrisy and prejudice, that Dusty sometimes had a short fuse. The ten tracks were recorded at the Sigma Sound Studios, Philadelphia, at the end of 1969 and the album released in America in January 1970—in England, it retained its original title and came out in January. It was a concept album of sorts, the first Dusty had done where all the songs came from the same team, headed by songwriter-producers Kenny Gamble and Leon Gamble, virtually unknown when they worked with her, though with her soul connections she had heard of them—they famously went on to work with the Three Degrees. Today, the album is regarded as a curiosity item with only hard core fans knowing most of the songs, a shame because it is quite good. 'Joe' is one of the nicest she performed at this time, as is 'Let's Talk It Over' which has her backed with a gospel-style choir, The Sweethearts of Sigma. Dusty should have had a major hit on her hands, but as the decade drew to a close, she was faced with an inconsolable dilemma. Philips were reluctant to promote her US releases while she was working in America for Atlantic, and vice-versa. Though most of her shows were sell-outs whichever side of the Atlantic she happened to be on, it was this constantly being in the wrong place at the wrong time which helped bring down the curtain on Dusty Springfield's commercial career when she was just thirty years old, though as an artiste she would shine until the very end.

Five: Ne me quitte pas...

'How can I be sure, in a world that's constantly changing?' Dusty asked, in September 1970. Written by Felix Cavaliere and Eddie Brigati, 'How Can I Be Sure?' had been introduced by The Young Rascals. Dusty had never heard of them or their version: during a trip to Paris she has heard Nicoletta singing the French version, 'Je ne pense qu'a t'aimer', on the juke box. Born in 1944, she had a similar voice to Dusty's. Ray Charles, who covered her 'Il est mort le soleil', said, 'There are only two women alive today with black voices—Nicoletta and Dusty Springfield.' Someone called the chanteuse, and it was agreed that Dusty would be allowed to sing exactly the same arrangement, complete with accordions. As such it is one of her finest interpretations. She promoted it on *The Morecambe & Wise Show*, and the record reached Number 35 in the charts and with more airplay almost certainly would have gone higher. Later there would be cover versions by David Cassidy and Gloria Estefan, neither of which even remotely compare with the Dusty and Nicoletta versions.

Sadly, Dusty's world was already changing. In a musical environment where success was measured in revolutions per minute, her fabulous hit-parade run had more or less ended after less than a decade. Had she readily accepted this, as most of her middle-of-the-road contemporaries had been compelled to, she might have survived better over the next thirty years. Tom Jones, Peggy Lee, Sinatra, Vikki Carr, Kathie Kirby, Engelbert Humperdinck, Sandie Shaw and dozens more rarely enjoyed chart success once the Seventies dawned, yet they were no less successful on the cabaret-theatre circuit. Most too became album stars, selling many more copies than the so-called megastars of today—without *getting* into the charts. Edith Piaf and Nana

Mouskouri, who each had just one chart entry in Britain, have at the time of writing sold over 450 million albums between them. For Dusty, more popular than ever with audiences at this time, it was almost as if it had to be the charts or nothing at all.

Her third album for Atlantic, *Faithful*, was abandoned—the aborted material would be added to the 1999 reissue of *Dusty In Memphis*. The next one, *See All Her Faces*, was released in Britain only. Its successor, *Cameo*, was released in the US on the ABC Dunhill label in 1973 and despite above average material from the pens of Melissa Manchester, Barry Manilow, and Barry Mann and Cynthia Weill received virtually no airplay or mention in the music press. Dusty hated making it. 'They wanted me to record material *they* had selected,' she told *Billboard*. 'I was terribly galled that they'd done some tracks without even asking me what key. I became terribly uncooperative and dug in my heels. I wanted out.' Dorothy Squires, who she had met through their mutual friend Danny La Rue—the two even swapped dresses!—told me, 'Most of the songs Dusty was forced to sing in those days were second rate. A singer has her own particular style which she likes to stick to. They wouldn't have got away with telling Bassey or myself what to sing. Dusty was too soft with them.'

Critics observed that some of the songs had been given portentous titles: 'Mixed Up Girl', 'Let Me Down Easy', 'Nothing Is Forever', 'Girls It Ain't Easy', and her flawless reading of Aznavour's 'Yesterday When I Was Young' which was given pride of place in her opening night at the Talk of The Town on 4 December. Dusty had the flu, and was advised by her doctor to cancel. Bernard Delfont would not hear of this: she struggled valiantly through an excellent 65-minute set, coughing and sipping water between songs and even gave a couple of encores. The next morning, she received a call from Harold Fielding, the first of many managers during her 'wilderness' years: the rest of the four-week season had been cancelled. Dusty sued Delfont for £10,000 in lost earnings.

Things appeared to be looking up when Dusty recorded Glen Larson and Stu Philips' theme for two *Six-Million Dollar Man* television movies. Her voice was in tremendous form, and it was a pretty good tune. Only the lyrics were naff. At around the same time she began work on her second ABC Dunhill album, but the sessions were inexplicably abandoned. Some of this material would be released on the 2001 compilation, *Beautiful Soul*.

Having ended her relationship with Norma Tanega, Dusty relocated to Los Angeles—she said to get away from the British tabloids, always on the lookout for exclusives on her private life. Speaking to Ray Connolly of London's *Evening Standard*, and in an act which was totally out of character, in 1970 she had confessed to being promiscuous and bemoaned the guilt this brought, adding, 'I don't leap into bed with someone new every night, but I can be very unfaithful. It's fun while it's happening, but not fun afterwards because I'm filled with self-recrimination.' In 1973, speaking to the *Los Angeles Free Press* she, who had always been cautious and paranoid about being outed by the press, opted to come clean:

> I mean, people say that I'm gay, gay, gay, gay, gay, gay, gay, gay. I'm not anything. I basically want to be straight. I go from men to women and I don't give a shit. The catchphrase is: I can't love a man. Now, that's my hang-up. To love, to go to bed—fantastic. But to love a man is my prime ambition. They frighten me!

That was that, making one wonder what all the 'Is-she-or-isn't-she" fuss had been about. Nothing had changed—she was still the same Dusty!

The newspapers reported tales of drug abuse and alcohol dependency, hospitalisations and self-harming episodes. Friends who stuck by her while she was alive have since her death recounted drinking binges and 'cutting' incidents which they believed to have been inextricably linked to the attention-seeking hand-burning of her childhood. They have spoken of suicide attempts, slashed wrists, overdoses, and threats to fling herself off balconies. Some of these things actually happened, but some were 'buffered up' to appear more serious than they really were. Dusty certainly went through a very bad patch in 1983, becoming a victim of domestic violence which resulted in doctors temporarily declaring her a manic depressive. In April of this year, at an Alcoholics Anonymous meeting in Los Angeles, she fell in with an unsavoury crowd and struck up a friendship with Teda Bracci, a vivacious but unstable brunette bit-part actress seven years her junior who had recently played a mental patient in the film, *Frances*, a depressing saga if ever there was one, telling the story of lobotomised movie star Frances Farmer. The relationship developed, and seven months later the couple 'married' at the San Fernando ranch of Helene Sellery, another AA member—the party guests were all from an infamous local rehab centre. Dusty, the bride, in a rare moment of lapsed fashion sense wore a floor-length 'chez Oxfam' white meringue gown and white silk Stetson, while the 'groom' wore black. Their first row occurred during the journey home, when the now-teetotal Dusty learned that Bracci had sneaked a bottle of champagne into the reception. Their last was not long afterwards when, apparently, after several nasty assaults by her partner she was hospitalised after Bracci smashed her in the face with a saucepan, badly injuring her cheek and knocking out several teeth. Not to be outdone, Dusty hit her over the head with a skillet—exit Teda Bracci. She told Kris Kirk:

> I was beaten up more than once by the same person, and the second time I experienced what battered wives often come up against, where they're afraid to talk because they'll get beaten up again. But the relationship was so disapproved of anyway that people turned round and said, 'We told you so, you should never have married her in the first place.' I've been through it and if I can do anything to help there, I will.

Plastic surgery, performed at the Cedars Sinai Hospital, gave Dusty a new look: her face emerged thinner, almost emaciated at first, her cheekbones, chin and nose more pronounced. She had also ditched most of her wigs, and cut down on the mascara—the black stuff which she once said she hardly ever washed off had been eschewed for a more subtle deep purple and magenta. In America, she became involved with several refuges for battered women, performing in charity concerts to raise funds—this was when she was not raising money for her animal charities, including one which rescued kodiak bears. At this trying time she also provided backing vocals for 'Snowbird' songstress Anne Murray's album, *Together*, and Elton John's *Caribou*.

In 1978, Dusty entered the Cherokee Studios, in West Hollywood to cut *It Begins Again* for Atlantic. The album was produced by Roy Thomas Baker, though for Dusty things would not be beginning again for a while. Her 1979 UK album, *Living Without Your Love*, fared slightly better, but still did not chart. Philips promoted it as her comeback release, though she was quick to remind journalists that she had not been anywhere. Neither, she said, was doing it for the money. 'If I had to do it for that alone, I'd breed cats,' she snapped at one reporter. Again, some of the songs were portentous and most especially appreciated by her legion of gay fans: 'Be Somebody', 'Closet Man', 'Save Me, Save Me'—and 'I'm Coming Home Again'.

This was another year of mixed fortunes. Sell-out concerts at London's Drury Lane Theatre were followed by provincial cancellations owing to poor advertising and therefore poor ticket sales. Though distressed about this, Dusty made light of the situation, appearing on the BBC's *Pebble Mill At One* wearing her 'funeral' attire of Portuguese *fadista*'s black veil. At the end of the year, she gave a spectacular concert at London's Royal Albert Hall, one of her finest later recitals, if not the finest of her career. Piaf had done *Olympia 60,* Judy Garland *Carnegie Hall 61*, Dorothy Squires *Palladium 70*. All had been recorded for posterity, and sold millions of copies worldwide. All had taken place in the wake of extreme adversity—Dusty's too, for it was the day before her father's funeral, and when she was still getting over losing her mother to lung cancer. O.B. had been died of a suspected heart-attack at his home.

The Royal Albert Hall concert constituted a charity performance, in front of a frosty and very rude Princess Margaret, on behalf of the Invalid Children's Aid Society. Introduced by a sneering, condescending Russell Harty, Dusty bounced on to the stage wearing a sparkling white top and trousers, and opened with 'I Close My Eyes And Count To Ten'. Next up was 'We Are Family' in which she emphasised the line, 'All my sisters and me!' Around 90 per cent of the capacity crowd were gay, and Dusty played to these, as did the camera, completely ignoring the royal patron. All the big hits were there, each greeted with a bigger storm of applause than the last, and inasmuch as the fans were not interested in Princess Margaret, neither was Dusty. The crunch came after 'All I See Is You' when Dusty quite innocuously pronounced, 'It's nice to see that all the royalty is not confined to the royal box!' The Princess was not amused and walked out—returning after what one member of the theatre's staff described as 'a fag and gin break' to catch the last two songs. Here, Dusty had her revenge when she glanced up and saw the Princess chatting to her lady-in-waiting. Disappearing into the wings for a lightning change into a beautiful tailed lilac trouser-suit, she walked back on and, stepping over a carpet of multicoloured carnations, began her penultimate song, 'Quiet please—there's a lady on the stage!' This was not just her tribute to all the great tragic female singers of the past, but Dusty's inadvertent way of telling this other lady to shut up and not be so ignorant—that the lady standing in the spotlight might be past her best, but that she was still entitled to respect. This display of bad manners continued in the wings when Margaret congratulated everyone who had been involved with the production—and arrogantly strode straight past Dusty, whose manager had just handed her a cheque for the £8,000 which Dusty had raised!

There was more. The next day, Dusty received a letter from St James' Palace—pre-typed, purporting to be from Princess Margaret herself and including an apology for the 'insults' Dusty had levelled at the Queen, with a space for her signature! Such was Dusty's naivety that she signed the paper and returned it. The show had been taped for broadcast over the Christmas period, but the BBC dropped it from their schedule. The hilarious end to this upsetting episode was recalled by Dusty's biographer, Sharon Davis, in 2008: 'Known by the nickname Yvonne in the gay fraternity, a news item in the *Daily Mail* in 2007 suggested that Princess Margaret "was rumoured to have had affairs with lovers including Peter Sellers and, more improbably, Dusty Springfield."'

Neither was it the first time that Dusty had 'offended' royalty: the previous year she had jokingly told *Gay News*, 'I'm having a three-way with Princess Anne and one of her horses.'

Had Dusty taken a leaf out of the Piaf-Judy-Squires book and concentrated on giving great performances instead of worrying about record sales, her career might have recovered to reach unprecedented heights, as had happened when Dorothy Squires had hired the Palladium in 1970, after being snubbed for years by the establishment. In 1981 she signed a contract in the US with 20th Century Records, and the following year released an album, *White Heat*. Most fans were more interested in the sleeve than the content: the reverse depicted her wearing a motorcycle helmet, it was alleged at the time to conceal the bruises inflicted by Teda Bracci. Arguably the worst album she ever made, the record company's attempts to use Dusty to cash in on the current Hi Energy gay disco craze which even the sultry Eartha Kitt had conquered, it was just another flop.

In 1985, Dusty returned to the UK, where she gave the previously mentioned interview for the *Daily Express*'s acid-tongued columnist Jean Rook, who observed with her customary lack of tact, 'At first startling glance, she looks like a terrorist with a built-in hood. Or an ancient Greek death mask. Her mouth is a blood red gash. Her make-up looks bullet-proof.' And top of Rook's agenda: Dusty's sexuality. To say that the interview was an ordeal was an understatement though there would be more to come during this visit to Britain. Hippodrome owner Peter Stringfellow had assigned her to a £100,000 one-album-three-singles deal with his Hippodrome Records label, along with engagements at his clubs up and down the country—ending with a season at the Hippodrome itself, a mecca for the gay community. The most he got in the end was a one-off television appearance on the BBC's *Wogan*, promoting her new single, 'Sometimes Like Butterflies'. This had originally featured on the flipside of Donna Summer's 'Finger On The Trigger', and for a woman whose fan-base was so predominantly gay, the last thing Dusty wanted was to be associated with a woman who had publicly declared that AIDS was God's punishment on gay men, a statement which almost irreparably damaged Summer's career.

'I think Peter and I make an explosive combination,' Dusty said at the time, though when the record flopped and she returned to America with her tail tucked firmly between her legs, she was singing a different tune.

'Peter knew fuck all about the record industry,' she told a waiting press conference. 'My relationship with him was one of the incidents that made me so fed up with the business, I nearly gave it up for good.'

Stringfellow defended himself by saying that this was indeed true, that he knew very little about the record industry—but enough to know that it was impossible for any artiste to have a hit with a record they refused to promote, as Dusty had done. And the problem had of course arisen over the *choice* of record, which had been Dusty's decision alone.

The tabloids, and even Dusty herself at times, were suggesting that maybe she was all washed up. Then, in 1987, when Vicki Wickham took over as her manager, came an offer to work with the Pet Shop Boys, an idea originally suggested by Peter Stringfellow—and impolitely dismissed. This time the opportunity came by way of Neil Tennant, a fervent Dusty fan, who asked her to duet with them on their new single, 'What Have I Done To Deserve This?', and also appear in the promotional video. The record reached Number 2 in the British and US charts, though whether by way of actual merit, or on account of its curiosity value may be a matter for conjecture. With the flat, tuneless voices of Tennant and Chris Lowe, and with Dusty only slightly improving matters with her 'Since you went away' segments, it was vastly inferior to her recent failed singles—though her subsequent work with the Pet Shop Boys would show a marked improvement when their voices were kept out of the proceedings.

'I'm really grateful to the Pet Shop Boys, she said in a BBC Radio One interview. 'And I feel embarrassed to say that. It sticks in my craw to be grateful, but I am because they had the faith in me that I didn't have.'

Much better was Dusty's duet, 'Something In Your Eyes', with an inaudible Richard Carpenter for his *Time* album, Carpenter's first solo outing since the death of his sister Karen. The single reached Number 12 in the US Adult Contemporary Chart. The promotional video was also interesting: Dusty lip-synchs the song while leaning, Judy-style, against the upright piano. She also recorded a duet with B J Thomas: 'As Long As We Got Each Other' was the theme from the American sitcom, *Growing Pains*. Then, in January 1988 she hit the jackpot when Philips put out *The Silver Collection*, a much-publicised and applauded retrospective of her halycon days. Within a month of its release, the 22-track album achieved gold status, bringing the comment from *Melody Maker*, 'If Dusty Springfield didn't exist, it would naturally be necessary to invent her.'

The album's success prompted Dusty to leave America for good. Unable to bring her cats to Britain because of the strict quarantine laws, she relocated to Holland where this was possible, renting a cramped flat in Amsterdam. Zipping back and forth to London she appeared on numerous chat shows, setting a precedent by always having a friend close at hand. Toying nervously with her fingers, she would persistently glance to the wings—which she admitted she could not see on account of her acute myopia—as if in search of approval that the interview was going well. One with Clive Anderson went badly. Anderson seemed interested only in drawing attention to himself and his non-funny jokes, while the (unseen) props man instructed the audience when to laugh, and Dusty refused to sing. 'Never again,' she said afterwards. Michael Aspel, on the other hand, coaxed out of her a rip-roaring 'I Only Want To Be With You', treated her (as indeed he treated all his guests) kindly and with respect, and she reciprocated with unusual candour when asked about her recent addictions:

> There's nothing funny about a drunken woman, and nothing funny about a very stoned woman....I wouldn't recommend joining that particular club. [Stopping] is not a matter of willpower, it's just a matter of finding that you dislike yourself so much and you're behaving like a complete creep. Some people never realise that about themselves....It's very easy to stop drinking and doing drugs. It's not easy to stay stopped.

In February 1989, Dusty released her second, technically and vocally more satisfactory collaboration with the Pet Shop Boys. 'Nothing Has Been Proved' was used as the soundtrack of the film, *Scandal*, which recounted the John Profumo-Christine Keeler-Mandy Rice Davies controversy which in 1963 brought down the Macmillan government. A lengthy record, this time she was given all the vocals (the Pet Shop Boys intermittently pronounced the word 'scandal') and it reached Number 16 in the UK charts, her first big solo hit since 1968's 'I Close My Eyes And Count To Ten'. As had happened with her Shirley Temple sketch, the promotional video showed Dusty, gloved and clad in purple, sporting a new spiky hairstyle while performing in front of monochrome newsreel footage of the Profumo affair. The single also saw her making a welcome return to *Top Of The Pops*, and an allegedly not so welcome reunion with *Ready, Steady, Go!*'s Cathy McGowan, who asked her during a local television news report, "What does it feel like to be a superstar again?" As if she had ever been anything else!

'Nothing Has Been Proved' was one of the tracks on Dusty's new album, *Reputation*, released in June 1990—her first for Parlophone. Part-produced by the Pet Shop Boys, it had been recorded over an 18-months period and peaked at Number 38 in the charts, selling 80,000 copies in its first month. The second single from the album, 'In Private', reached Number 14. Dusty was back! She also returned to London, moving in with her secretary Pat Rhodes and her husband until she could find a place of her own—for the next six months, her preoccupation would be in ensuring that she never missed a day visiting her beloved cats, which were now in quarantine. Eventually, she moved into The Granary, part of the Frogmill Court complex at Hurley, in Berkshire.

Dusty hit the headlines in 1991 following a sketch in ITV's *The Bobby Davro Show* wherein the comic parodied her, wearing high heels and a cheap wig, staggering across the stage, swigging from a bottle while slurring the words to 'What Have I Done To Deserve This?' Dusty was upset, but would let the matter ride, had it not been for a call from

Dorothy Squires, who over the years had had more than her share of similar put-downs.

Dorothy told me, 'I said to her, "Sue the hell out of them, Dusty. Once you let these bastards get away with robbing you of your dignity, they just keep on doing it."'

Oddly, it was not Davro she sued but the television company. She had *had* a drink problem, she confessed, but for eight years now not one drop of alcohol had passed her lips. The court awarded her £75,000 in damages, and ordered ITV to make a public apology.

In October 1993, Dusty joined forces with Cilla Black, when Cilla was putting together an album celebrating her thirty years in show business. *Through The Years* was a collection of duets with friends and colleagues, and Dusty's contribution was *Heart & Soul*, which was also released as a single. The following year, Columbia this time put out what would be her final album, *A Very Fine Love*, produced by Tom Shapiro. Recorded in Nashville, where the Springfields had made their first American album, she had wanted to call it *Dusty In Nashville* but the record company talked her out of it, claiming that fans and the media would be expecting a country album. Released in the UK in June 1995, it just squeezed into the Top 40.

Dusty had been feeling run down for a while, and when she returned home from America she consulted her doctor, who discovered an abnormality in her breast. A specialist at the Royal Marsden Hospital discovered cancer—fairly advanced though not too far to affect a cure. She was immediately put on a course of chemotherapy, and the fact that this did not make her lose her hair or too much weight enabled her to keep her illness a secret from all but her very closest friends. The news finally hit the press in November 1994, by which time doctors at the Royal Marsden had given her an 'above average' chance of survival.

Dusty carried on working, promoting the new album. There were appearances on *The Edna Everage Show*, and on BBC2's *Later With Jools Holland*, where she plugged a new single, 'Where Is A Woman To Go?' Her 'backing singers' were fellow guests Sinead O'Connor and Alison Moyet. She made a fleeting appearance on ITV's breakfast programme, where she spoke candidly about her cancer diagnosis and thanked the Royal Marsden for looking after her. Not long afterwards, portentously performing George and Ira Gershwin's 'Someone To Watch Over Me', she appeared in a 60-seconds television commercial for life assurance. Her swansong was a taped a segment for *Des O'Connor Tonight*—some years earlier, they had clowned around while duetting on 'Messing About On The River'.

Early in 1996, Dusty's cancer returned with a vengeance. The disease had now spread to her bones. Over the next six months she underwent more chemotherapy, and for one known to favour looking on the black side fought valiantly from her corner. Her three closest friends—Pat Rhodes, Vicki Wickham and backing-singer Simon Bell—were asked to sign confidentiality agreements promising not to discuss her illness, or her private life after her death. Wickham would subsequently pen a kiss-and-tell, *Dancing With Demons*. Dusty began planning her funeral. A lapsed Catholic, she wanted to atone by having a priest officiate at her service, after which she would be privately cremated— her ashes would be divided into two urns, one to be interred within the local churchyard so that fans could visit, the other to be scattered into the Atlantic from one of her favourite beauty spots, the Cliffs of Moher, in County Clare. Her possessions would be sold and the proceeds donated to friends and animal charities. In the meantime, to ensure that she would have the very best in medical care, she assigned her future royalties to the Prudential Insurance

Company for £1.25 million—effectively a loan which in time would be paid back.

Dusty's friends fiercely protected her from the outside world, inasmuch as her fans only learned how ill she really was in February 1998 was when she failed to turn up at the BRITs, where she was to have presented Icelandic singer Bjork with an award. Within hours, dozens of reporters were camped in the forecourt outside her Berkshire home, along with hundreds of anxious fans. There was no question of Dusty staying here now, and shortly afterwards she moved into a large rented house set in extensive grounds at Harpsden Bottom, Henley-on-Thames. The property was enclosed by an electric fence, assuring her of complete privacy.

On 14 April, two days before her 59th birthday, Dusty tuned in to the television news to learn that Dorothy Squires had died of lung cancer, Dusty, who still had one of Dorothy's dresses in her closet, sent flowers to the funeral. Three days later she received word that Paul McCartney's wife, Linda, had also succumbed to the disease.

In the May, doctors at the Royal Marsden gave Dusty just three months to live. Surrounded by friends and loved ones, she rallied a little and soldiered on for a good deal longer, so much so that fans switching on their radios in anticipation of hearing the worst came to the conclusion that, as before, she had been given the all clear. They realised this was not so when, on 30 December, her name was published in the New Year's Honours List. She, who had never held much faith with royalty since being snubbed by Princess Margaret, had been awarded the OBE. The grim news was that she might not live to personally collect the award from Buckingham Palace. Arrangements were therefore made for Vicki Wickham to collect it on her behalf and present it to her at the Royal Marsden.

A few days after receiving news of her OBE, Dusty returned to Henley. Refusing to sleep in her bedroom, between bouts of consciousness she held court in her living room. It was here, at 10.43 pm on Tuesday 2 March—the day she should have gone to Buckingham Palace, that she slipped away in her sleep.

Dusty's funeral, on Friday 12 March 1999, befitted the noble person she had been—a day which, with her sense of humour, would have amused her because it was Red Nose Day. She had jokingly remarked how she had wanted to stop the traffic and bring Henley to a standstill, and this is exactly what happened. The town centre was cordoned off as hundreds of fans arrived to pay their last respects. In the drizzle, some fell to their knees behind the crash-barriers, to which had been attached tiny bunches of wild flowers. The celebrity mourners included Dusty's brother Tom, Lulu, the Pet Shop Boys, Madeleine Bell, Julie Felix and Kiki Dee. Floral tributes were sent by Cilla Black, Sandie Shaw, The Rolling Stones, and Burt Bacharach.

Years before, a friend had showed Dusty footage of Mario Lanza's funeral in Rome where his casket had made its way through the streets in a glass-sided antique carriage, drawn by liveried black horses. Anyone visiting Henley, not knowing what had happened, might have been excused for thinking that the crowds were saying farewell to a royal personage, and in a way they were. Within the carriage the name DUSTY was spelled out in pink and white flowers, and as the coffin was carried into the church Dusty's recording of 'You Don't Have To Say You Love Me' was relayed through loud speakers. Simon Bell sang 'The Wind Beneath My Wings'. For many, the most heartbreaking moment was when Dusty's voice rang out again as the coffin left the church to a loud applause from the crowd.

"I think I'm going back...

Dusty Springfield: 1960s Vinyl Discography

1963
I Only Want To Be With You/ Once Upon A Time
Philips BF1292

1964
Stay Awhile/ Something Special
Philips BF1313

I Only Want To Be With You: I Only Want To Be With You; He's Got Something; Twenty-Four Hours From Tulsa; Every Day I Have To Cry
(**EP**) Philips BE12560

A Girl Called Dusty: Mama Said; You Don't Own Me; Do Re Mi; When The Lovelight Starts Shining Thru His Eyes; My Colouring Book; Mockingbird; Twenty-Four Hours From Tulsa; Nothing; Anyone Who Had A Heart; Will You Love Me Tomorrow; Wishin' & Hopin'; Baby Don't You Know
(**LP**) Philips BL7594

I Just Don't Know What To Do With Myself/ My Colouring Book
Philips BF1348

Aud dich nur wart'ich immerzu/ Warten und hoffen
German release, no other details

Dusty: Can I Get A Witness; All Cried Out; Wishin' & Hopin'; I Wish I'd Never Loved You
(**EP**) Philips BE12564

Tento so che poi mi passa/ Stupido, stupido
Italian release, no other details

Losing You/ Summer Is Over
Philips BF1369

Tu che ne sai/ Di fronte all'amore   (Italian release, details)

O Holy Child/ Jingle Bells (with The Springfields)
Philips BF1381

1965
Your Hurtin' Kinda Love/ Don't Say It Baby
Philips BF1396

Dusty In New York: Live It Up; I Want Your Love Tonight; I Wanna Make You Happy; Now That You're My Baby
(**EP**) Philips 12572

In The Middle Of Nowhere/ Baby Don't You Know
Philips BF1418

Mademoiselle Dusty: Demain tu peux changer; L'été est fini; Je ne peux pas t'en vouloir; Reste encore un instant
(**EP**) Philips BE12579

Some Of Your Loving/ I'll Love You For A While
Philips BF1430

Everything's Coming Up Dusty: Won't Be Long; Oh No! Not My Baby; Long After Midnight Is All Over; La Bamba; Who Can I Turn To; Doodlin'; If It Don't Work Out; That's How Heartaches Are Made; It Was Easier To Hurt Him; I've Been Wrong Before; I Can Hear You; I Had A Talk With My Man; Packin' Up
(**LP**) Philips RBL10024

1966
Little By Little/ If It Hadn't Been For You
Philips BF1466

You Don't Have To Say You Love Me/ Every Ounce Of Strength
Philips BF1482

Goin' Back/ I'm Gonna Leave You
Philips BF1502

All I See Is You/ Go Ahead On
Philips BF1510

Golden Hits: I Only Want To Be With You; I Just Don't Know What To Do With Myself; In The Middle Of Nowhere; Losin' You' All Cried Out; Some Of Your Lovin'; Wishin' & Hopin'; My Colouring Book; Little By Little; You Don't Have To Say You Love Me; Goin' Back; All I See Is You
(**LP**) Philips BL7737

1967
I'll Try Anything/ The Corrupt Ones
Philips BF1553

Give Me Time/ The Look Of Love
Philips BF1577

What's It Gonna Be/ Small Town Girl
Philips BF1608

Where Am I Going: Bring Him Back; Don't Let Me Lose This Dream; I Can't Wait Until I See My Baby's Face; Take Me For A Little While; Chained To A Memory; Sunny; They Long To Be Close To You; Welcome Home; Come Back To Me; If You Go Away; Broken Blossoms; Where Am I Going
(**LP**) Philips BL7820

1968
I Close My Eyes And Count To Ten/ No Stranger Am I
Philips BF1682

If You Go Away: If You Go Away; Magic Garden; Sunny; Where Am I Going
(**EP**) Philips BE12605

Dusty Springfield: Twenty-Four Hours From Tulsa; Anyone Who Had A Heart; Go Ahead On; Every Day I Have To Cry; Now That You're My Baby; The Corrupt Ones; The Look Of Love; Live It Up; I Wish I'd Never Loved You; Reste encore un instant; Who Can I Turn To; I Want Your Love Tonight
(LP) World Record Club T848

I Will Come To You/ The Colour Of Your Eyes
Philips BF1706

Dusty Definitely: Ain't No Sun Since You've Been Gone; Take Another Little Piece Of My Heart; Another Night; Mr Dream Merchant; I Can't Give Back The Love I Feel For You; Love Power; This Girl's In Love With You; I Only Want To Laugh; Who Will Take My Place; I Think It's Gonna Rain Today; Morning; Second Time Around
(LP) Philips SBL7864

Son Of A Preacher Man/ Just A Little Lovin'
Philips BF1730

Stay Awhile: I Only Want To Be With You; Stay Awhile; Mama Said; Anyone Who Had A Heart; When The Lovelight Starts Shining Thru His Eyes; Wishin' & Hopin'; Mockingbird; You Don't Own Me; Something Special; Every Day I Have To Cry
(LP) Wing WL1211

1969
Dusty In Memphis: Just A Little Lovin'; So Much Love; Son Of A Preacher Man; I Don't Want To Hear It Any More; Don't Forget About Me; Breakfast In Bed; Just One Smile; The Windmills Of Your Mind; In The Land Of Make Believe; No Easy Way Down; I Can't Make It Alone
(LP) Philips SBL7889

Am I The Same Girl/ Earthbound Girl
Philips BF1811

Brand New Me/ Bad Case Of The Blues
Philips BF1826

1970 (recorded 1969)
From Dusty....With Love: Lost; Bad Case Of The Blues; Never Love Again; Let Me Get In Your Way; Let's Get Together Soon; Brand New Me; Joe; Silly Fool; The Star Of My Show; Let's Talk It Over
(**LP**) Philips SBL7927

Helen Shapiro

Teenager Sings The Blues

Many regarded her as something of a novelty, a flash in the pan. She was certainly much more than that, though her chart life was fairly brief: hitting the dizzy heights of success in 1961, she enjoyed two chart-toppers and eight Top 40 hits. Three years later, her commercial career was all but over—much less to do with lack of talent, which she possessed in bundles, than in the direction the British music scene was taking with the advent of Mersey Mania. Had she emerged a little later, she might have achieved the same level of long-lasting fame as a Cilla, a Dusty or a Marianne.

    The descendent of Russian Jewish immigrants who had settled in London's East End, Helen Shapiro was born at the

Bethnal Green Hospital on 28 September 1946. Hers was a musical family: her mother, Rachel, played the violin and her father, Barney, is said to have been possessed of a fine singing voice. The Shapiros—grandparents, aunts and uncles, cousins—all lived within a few streets of each other. Most were involved with the tailoring business and, though far from wealthy, appear to have been a happy and contented group who worked hard and who, like most close-knit Jewish families, frequently got together once the shutters came down for a good old-fashioned shindig. The religious festivals were especially exciting because these brought in relatives from further afield. No one possessed a record player, and aside from the wireless this was their main source of entertainment. Helen's favourites in these days were stalwarts Bing Crosby, Doris Day and Rosemary Clooney, along with Jewish institutions Al Jolson and Sophie Tucker.

'I have fond memories of my childhood,' she recalled. 'Nobody ever had the chance to get big-headed. It was drilled into us from a very early age that musical talent was a gift from God. In a family so talented. who were we to argue?'

Helen had an older brother, Ronnie (born 1942) with whom she shared a room in the cramped upper storey of a terraced house in Reighton Road, Upper Clapton. There were no facilities, so if anyone wanted to take a bath they had to drag out the tin tub and fill it from the copper boiler in the kitchen—otherwise it meant taking a trip to the public baths in nearby Hackney. At five, Helen was enrolled at Northwood Road School where, from a tender age, she learned to cope with anti-Semitism: the establishment was in the heart of the Jewish community, with around a quarter of the pupils belonging to the faith, so she never felt isolated. At seven, she joined the Clapton

Jewish Youth Club: Ronnie was already a member, and music was frequently on the agenda. Then in 1955 the Shapiros moved to a maisonette in Hackney's Rutland Road: this had three bedrooms so that Helen no longer had to share, a bathroom, and a small garden. Within walking distance was a cinema where she and her mother would watch the latest Hollywood musicals. She had made up her mind already that she wanted to be a singer. Also, by now her taste in music had changed: she was into Bill Haley, Elvis Presley, Neil Sedaka—and Cliff Richard, who later became a friend. Sometimes she and her pals would hang around outside the stage door of the Hackney Empire. Her proudest moment in those days, she said, was getting Marty Wilde's autograph.

In 1957, Helen, her brother and a group of friends from the youth club—one was lorry driver's son Mark Feld, who later became Marc Bolan—formed their own band. Their repertoire comprised the chart hits of the day, but with an emphasis on skiffle. Helen also developed a passion for entering talent contests, whenever she and her family went to Westcliff or Margate—invariably walking off with first prize. When skiffle started to go out of fashion, she and Ronnie turned to jazz—her field of expertise later in life. How she came about her unusual voice—basso profundo, even at the age of eleven—is a matter for conjecture, most likely a combination of ancestry and very early smoking. She confesses in her memoirs that, at junior school, she liked nothing more than sneaking into the playground toilets to light up.

Helen's quest for fame came about courtesy of her Uncle Harry, who saw an advertisement in the local paper for the grandly-titles Maurice Burman School of Pop Singing. Burman, whose offices were in Bickenhall Mansions, at the junction of Baker Street and Marylbone Road, had formerly been a drummer with Geraldo's orchestra. Besides running his academy he wrote a column for *Melody Maker*. His fees—25 shillings for four hours tuition on Saturday mornings—were steep, but if the talent was there his success rate was high. He had helped Alma Cogan when she had been starting out.

Helen had been with Burman's academy for a month before she met the man himself. Burman was so impressed with her raw, as yet untrained talent that when Uncle Harry, paying for the lessons, asked how she was shaping up, Burman told him that from now on her fee would be wavered because in his estimation she had reached the point where she should be considered for a recording contract. A few days later, Helen auditioned for John Barry, who had written for Adam Faith and later composed for the Bond movies. Barry knocked her back, but not to be outdone, Burman encouraged her to keep up the lessons.

A few months later, Helen was placed under the tutelage of John Schroeder, then assistant to the conductor Norrie Paramor, who doubled as A & R executive producer for Columbia Records. Paramor (1914-79), a former MD with Ralph Reader's Gang Show and pianist with Harrie Gold, will go down in history for producing a wide range of number one singles and albums. Figuring among his greatest successes were Ruby Murray ('Softly, Softly'), Michael Holliday ('The Story Of My Life'), Eddie Calvert ('Oh Mein Papa'), Cliff Richard ('Living Doll') and Amália Rodrigues (*On Broadway*).

Schroeder auditioned Helen at Abbey Road. She put her heart and soul into 'Birth Of The Blues', as would later happen when she recorded the piece, and Schroeder later observed, 'She had a very jazzy voice, very deep, like a boy. Her timing, her phrasing and her whole presence was extremely strong—right in your face, I couldn't believe it!'

Schroeder played the acetate to Norrie Paramor, who also initially thought she was a boy. Helen sang for him, and was told that an initial six-months recording contract was hers for the taking. The only condition was that, as a minor, her parents would have to sign on her behalf.

For five of these months, Columbia deliberated over Helen's debut single, until finally they had to let her record something, or release her from her contract. Commercially, she was an 'in-between'—too young for romantic ballads in the stamp of Joan Regan, too mature for juvenile ditties. Neither did they want her to cover an American pop song as way too many British singers were doing this already. Paramor decided that something would have to be written especially for her, and gave the job to John Schroeder and Mike Hawker. The result was 'Don't Treat Me Like A Child', a good song marred only by the squeaky *yeah-yeahs* of the female backing singers. To create a gimmick, though she was against the idea, Helen was photographed in her school uniform—strumming a banjo. This song and the flipside, Maurice Burman's catchy 'When I'm With You', were recorded at Abbey Road with session musicians from the Ted Heath Band. Both tracks, like most of Helen's future recordings (which makes her along with Kathy Kirby almost unique in British pop) were laid down in a single take. 'I didn't get nervous,' she recalled. 'I just did what I knew how to do. Mum and Dad probably felt more nervous than I did.'

Helen cut the record in January 1961. and it was rush-released the following month. The Shapiros still did not own a record player—a problem which would soon be solved by the ever-benevolent Uncle Harry—so in order to listen to it, everyone had to nip around to a neighbour's house. Helen then resumed her 'normal' life—school, and swotting for her exams. Life, of course, would never be the same again. 'Don't Treat Me Like A Child' entered the charts, stalled at Number 28, then dropped out. Early in May, she was invited to appear on the pilot of television's *Thank Your Lucky Stars*: topping the bill was Michael Holliday. Introduced by Keith Fordyce, and with no other song to offer, she performed this one. Within a week it had re-entered the charts, and this time shot to Number 3. Suddenly, Britain had a new major talent, though Helen did not feel much like celebrating. That same week, her mentor Maurice Burman succumbed to cancer.

Burman's widow, Jean, and Norrie Paramor's brother Alan shared the handling of Helen's career. Jean taught her the art of presentation—how to dress and apply make-up, how to move on stage and rid herself of the wooden stance one sees in her early filmed performances. Paramor saw to her engagements: as she was still attending school, for now these were restricted to weekends and holidays. These early shows saw her emulating Alma Cogan's dress style: hooped skirts under which she wore yards and yards of tulle. Away from the spotlight, she liked to dress like any fashionable young woman—sloppy-Joe pullovers, slacks or tight skirts, and winkle-picker shoes.

Helen was promoted as 'The British Brenda Lee, quite simply because Columbia had no one else to compare her with. She was of course nothing like Brenda Lee—or Connie Francis, the only other female singer in the charts while 'Don't Treat Me Like A Child' was in the Top Ten, with whom comparisons were also made. Then for a little while, the press awarded her the somewhat unflattering moniker, 'Foghorn'. This was how she was affectionately known by her youth club band mates, though the tabloids used it only as a form of derision.

Unlike any other pop star who had enjoyed a major hit, Helen's schoolgirl status prevented her from doing much in the way of live performances. She was permitted to sing on Radio Luxembourg's *EMI Spectaculars*, hosted by Muriel Young and broadcast during the early evening. The BBC only had its Light Programme in those days, and Luxembourg was the only station which played 'young' music. The press, once they discovered that Helen was not a boy, made endless comparisons with Cliff Richard, claiming that she looked like him—in early photographs, the resemblance is uncanny. She met all her pop heroes—Cliff, Bobby Vee, Frank Ifield, Adam Faith—but confessed to having crushes on stars she had yet to meet, such as Paul Anka and Paul Newman. At fifteen she had a regular boyfriend, but the promoters at Columbia asked her to keep the romance low-key. It remained so until they split up, whence the tabloids made up the story that her parents had brought it to a halt. Away from the television, radio or recording studio, Helen tried to live her life as she had before fame beckoned—still going to the youth club once a week, or relaxing at home with her family.

Helen's second single was John Schroeder and Mike Hawker's 'You Don't Know', an engaging exercise in teen angst and completely different from its predecessor. Simply but effectively orchestrated by Martin Slavin and with its fair share of *'woah-woah-woahs'* this time, it topped the charts for three weeks in the late autumn of 1961. It remained in the Top 40 for five months—making Helen, at 14 years and 316 days, the youngest ever female artiste to have had a Number One—though the youngest, per se, had been Frankie Lymon, one year younger than Helen when his 'Why Do Fools Fall In Love' had topped the UK charts in 1956. On the flipside of Helen's record, which sold 500,000 copies and earned her her first Silver Disc, Columbia had plumped for Norrie Paramor and drag-queen

Bunny Lewis's 'Marvellous Lie', which if anything was even *better* than the A-side.

Suddenly, Helen was appearing in all the television pop shows of the day—*Oh, Boy!*, *Thank Your Lucky Stars*, *Juke Box Jury*—and making live appearances with the Shadows, Joe Brown, the Tremeloes, and the Temperance Seven. She was promoted as top of the bill, but because of her age not permitted to work Sundays, or to close the show because of the 10 pm curfew imposed by the entertainment rules of the day. Foreign tours meant she had to be chaperoned—in Europe by her mother, further afield by both parents. Her biggest engagement saw her supporting Dorothy Squires at Chester's Royalty Theatre. 'We were told to expect this archetypal little Shirley Temple prima donna,' Dorothy told me. 'But she was such a sweet little thing, polite, well aware of what she wanted out of her career, and so tremendously talented. I adored her!'

Helen's third single, released in September 1961 is the song which will always be associated with her, annoyingly so, she has said (though in 1993 she used it as the title for her memoirs) in that some think it to have been the *only* song she *ever* sang. 'Walkin' Back To Happiness', written by her by now regular team of Schroeder and Hawker, subsequently won them an Ivor Novello Award, yet initially she disliked it. 'It reminded me of "Campdown Races",' she recalled, adding that she much preferred the B-side, Norrie Paramor's 'Kiss N Run'. The *'woah-woahs"* were now replaced by *'woopah-oh-yeah-yeahs'*, and this one topped the charts for three weeks before being toppled by Elvis Presley's 'Little Sister'. Much was expected of the American release, but the record only reached Number 100 in the *Billboard* chart. While it was riding high in the British charts, Helen celebrated her fifteenth birthday at London's Talk of the Town—not performing, but as a guest at Dorothy Squires' opening night as the first non-American act to top the bill there.

Soon afterwards, Helen left school, and a few weeks later headed the bill on television's *Sunday Night At The London Palladium*. In November, she flew to Paris where she performed two songs in the first half of the Georges Brassens' recital at the Olympia. 'You Don't Know' had proved a hit in France, and 'Walkin' Back To Happiness' had just entered the French Top 40. She also recorded the song phonetically in German, and topped the charts with it in Japan. Later, she would successfully tour Australasia, South Africa, Israel, and make a lightning trip to New York where she appeared on Ed Sullivan's *Toast Of The Town*—an experience she claimed she had hated because of the host's rudeness and condescending attitude towards some of his guests. There would also be a two-week season at the Palladium with Matt Monro, whilst *Melody Maker* named her Top British Female Vocalist. The Variety Club of Great Britain awarded her their Silver Heart for Most Promising Newcomer.

For a couple of years, Helen Shapiro was sitting on top of the world. Her next single, released in February 1962, was Jeff Barry's 'Tell Me What He Said'. It reached Number 2 in the charts—kept from the top spot by The Shadows' 'Wonderful Land'. Next up was Norrie Paramor and Bunny Lewis's 'Let's Talk About Love', so short that it is almost over as soon as it begins. This reached a disappointing Number 23 in the charts. Helen sang it in the film, *It's Trad, Dad!* of which the least said the better. Directed by Richard (*Superman*) Lester, this also featured Craig Douglas, Gene Vincent, and Chubby Checker. Everyone played themselves in a scenario which sees a young couple campaigning to introduce the trad-jazz fad into their neighbourhood, when the oldies do not want it.

There would be an even worse follow-up movie, *Play It Cool*, directed by Michael Winner. Featuring Billy Fury, playing a character called Billy Universe, the singing was great but the acting dire. Helen performed two songs: 'I Don't Care' and 'Cry My Heart Out'. The former appeared on the B-side of Schroeder and Hawker's stunning teen-angst ballad, 'Little Miss Lonely', Helen's penultimate single of 1962, which peaked at Number 8 in the charts. Its successor was the raunchy 'Keep Away From Other Girls', but fans kept away from the record, which barely scraped into the Top 40. Almost certainly this would not have happened had she recorded it a few years later, for its composer was the then little-known Burt Bacharach. Columbia had scrapped the original demo which contained lyrics which see the impressionable girl criticising the smooth-talking seducer who has wooed her with, 'A hero sandwich and a glass of wine—a smile, a smoke, and oh such a great big line!' It was not considered appropriate for a teenage girl to advocate smoking, though Helen was fond of her tobacco, therefore 'smoke' was substituted by 'joke'.

Helen was singing better than ever and releasing records of supreme quality—Artie Wayne and Ben Raleigh's 'Queen For Tonight' was one of her best songs of 1963, and almost made the Top Thirty—but as the new year dawned, commercially it would all be downhill aside from 'No Trespassing', which topped the Australian charts. Her albums, excellent as these were, followed the same pattern, the exception being her first one, *Tops With Me*, released in 1962. This reached Number 2—a few hundred copies more and it would have occupied the top spot. Its successors, including *Helen's Sixteen* (the title was two-fold, sixteen tracks to coincide with her sixteenth birthday), and *Helen Hits Out!* did not chart, but contained some pretty eclectic material including a near-definitive version of "Basin Street

Blues" ultimately proving that jazz would always be Helen's first love.

Tops For Me saw Helen demonstrating her sheer versatilty, for it is representative of several very distinctive styles: pop, rock, chanson, jazz, scat and blues. There is the Shirelles' 'Will You Love Me Tomorrow?'—less strident and slower-paced than the original; a more than competent version of Elvis's 'Are You Lonesome Tonight?'; a not so good one of Marty Wilde's 'Teenager In Love'—by now, the teen-angst theme was starting to wear thin. From the French catalogue there was Gilbert Bécaud's 'The Day The Rains Came' (Le jour ou la pluie viendra) and Charles Trenet's 'Beyond The Sea' (La mer). Helen's stab at Connie Francis's 'Lipstick On Your Collar' and Brenda Lee's 'Sweet Nothin's' are way above average, and her take on Marv Johnson's 'You've Got What It Takes' may well be the first ever British cover of a Motown song.

At the end of 1962 Helen hit the road again, with The Beatles third on in a six-act bill and performing just four songs. The nationwide tour ticked off in Bradford, with Helen topping the bill and by now and actually staying to close the show. Within a few weeks, however, their roles were reversed when the group's 'Please Please Me' rocketed to Number 2 in the charts. Suddenly, in a strange twist of fate, The Beatles became all the rage and Helen was shunted aside—though she might not have slipped out of the charts so expediently had Columbia allowed her to record Misery', the song Lennon and McCartney penned for her at the time. Such a title, the company declared, was wholly unsuited for a teenager and the number was given to Kenny Lynch.

Helen's record sales plummeted in the aftermath of this tour. 'I'd been a novelty at fourteen but suffered from the Shirley Temple syndrome,' she remembered. 'I'd grown up.

Suddenly I was beginning to look a bit passé in spite of topping the bill.'

The quality of her material, on the other hand, only seemed to get better. In 1963, the year she ended her hugely successful run with Columbia, she pre-empted Dusty by proving that the likes of Dionne Warwick did not have a monopoly on Motown—many believe Helen's version of 'Walk On By' to have been far classier than Warwick's, and another gem was Berry Gordy's 'Shop Around'. Equally stunning was her cover of Carole King's 'It Might As Well Rain Until September'. The best interpretation of all would come in 1964 with her sassy cover version of Doris Day's 'Move Over Darling'—sexy and daring at the time for a 17-year-old promoted as the archetypal wholesome girl-next-door.

Also ahead of Dusty, and sadly not a success despite the contribution of the legendary saxophonist Boots Randolph, was Helen's Stateside-recorded album, *Helen In Nashville*. Her cover of Jackie DeShannon's 'Woe Is Me', taken from this, entered the *Billboard* Top 30, though the album itself failed to make much of an impression. Another great song on the album was 'It's My Party'. This track was earmarked for Helen's next single, but Columbia deliberated over it for so long that Mercury Records gazumped them and released the version by the then unknown Lesley Gore. The so-called 'brat song', produced by Quincy Jones and which gave the youth of America their latest buzz phrase, 'It's my party, and I'll cry if I want to,' topped the US charts and reached Number 9 in Britain.

Throughout the mid-Sixties, Helen continued touring home and abroad, travelling off the (then) beaten track as far afield as Poland and the Eastern bloc, Hong Kong, and the Philippines. She appeared regularly in pantomime and turned her attention to stage musicals. Her passion for jazz saw her championed by such legends as Humphrey Lyttleton. Still only eighteen, she was shortlisted to play Fanny Brice in the London production of *Funny Girl*, and doubtless would have excelled in the role—this was subsequently given to its creator, Barbra Streisand. At the end of 1969, Helen sang 'Walkin' Back To Happiness' in the BBC's *Pop Go The Sixties*. Appearing with her were Brit Girls Dusty, Cilla Black, Sandie Shaw, and Lulu.

Following appearances in several smaller theatrical productions, in 1979 Helen was cast in the role of Nancy—originally played by Georgia Brown—in the revival of Lionel Bart's *Oliver!* This played to capacity audiences in London's West End for almost a year. The reviews were excellent. Only the waspish Jean Rook found fault with her performance, denouncing her voice as sounding 'like a docker with laryngitis'. She also appeared in Willy Russell's adult comedy, *One For The Road*, and played Cynthia Lennon in television's surreal drama about the murdered Beatle, *A Journey In The Life*. This same year, 1985, she played hairdresser Viv Harker in Granada TV's twice-weekly soap, *Albion Market*. Arguably one of her biggest mistakes was accepting the part of Fantine in *Les Miserables*, only to back out of the production at the last minute—because she was moving home!

Helen's personal life has not always been so successful. In 1967, she married the promoter Duncan Weldon, five years her senior—this coincided with the release of a single, 'She Needs Company'. Her parents did not attend the ceremony: Weldon's father was Jewish, his mother so only by conversion. The marriage lasted but a few years. In 1971, Helen wed clothing manufacturer Morris Gundlash—this too failed. She is currently married to the actor John Judd, who she met while appearing in *Cabaret* in Lancaster. She has never had children.

In 1987, Helen became a Messianic Jew—one who believes in Christ as the Messiah. As such she has recorded several Messianic albums and, like her friend Cliff Richard, toured with her own gospel show.

And what, after half a century in the business, does Helen Shapiro regard as her greatest achievement in life? Her music? Her marriage? No, it is this latent religious revelation which she describes as, 'More important than the day I went to Maurice Burnam's school of pop singing, far more important than getting to Number One in the charts or appearing at the London Palladium, even more important than playing Nancy or making jazz records!'

Helen, with her friend Dorothy Squires.

Helen Shapiro: 1960s Vinyl Discography

1961
Don't Treat Me Like A Child/ When I'm With You (Columbia DB4589)

You Don't Know/ Marvellous Lie (Columbia DB4670)

Walkin' Back To Happiness/ Kiss N Run (Columbia DB4715)

1962
Tell Me What He Said/ I Apologise (Columbia DB4782)

Helen: Goody Goody; The Birth Of The Blues; Tiptoe Through The Tulips; After You've Gone (**EP**) Columbia SEG8128

Frag' mich nicht warum (Tell Me What He Said)/ Komm sei wieder gut (I Apologise) Sung in German. (Columbia C22038)

Let's Talk About Love/Sometime Yesterday (Columbia DB4824)

Den Ton kenn ich schon (Let's Talk About Love)/ Gestere nachmittag. Sung in German. Columbia C22130

Helen Shapiro's Hit Parade: Don't Treat Me Like A Child; You Don't Know; Walkin' Back To Happiness; When I'm With You (**EP**) Columbia SEG8136

Little Miss Lonely/ I Don't Care (Columbia DB4869)

'Tops' With Me: Little Devil; Will You Love Me Tomorrow; Because They're Young; The Day The Rains Came; Are You Lonesome Tonight; Teenager In Love; Lipstick On Your Collar; Beyond The Sea; Sweet Nothin's; You Mean Everything To Me; I Love You; You Got What It Takes
(**LP**) Columbia 33SX 1397/ SCX 3428

Keep Away From Other Girls/ Cry My Heart Out (Columbia DB4908)

Helen Shapiro: Parlons d'amour (Let's Talk About Love); Sans penser a rien (Sometime Yesterday); Tout ce qu'il vaudra (Tell Me What He Said); J'ai tant de remords (I Apologise) (**EP**) Columbia ESDF 1427 Sung in French

Parlons d'amour/ J'ai tant de remords (Columbia SCRF556)

Tout de qu'il voudra/ Sans penser a rien (Columbia SCRF557)

A Teenager Sings The Blues: A Teenager Sings The Blues; Blues In The Night; St Louis Blues (**EP**) Columbia SEG8170

Parlons d'amour/ Sans penser a rien (Columbia CL166021B)

Tout ce qu'il vaudra/ J'ai tant de remords (Columbia 166121B)

More Hits From Helen: Tell Me What He Said; I Apologise; Let's Talk About Love; Sometime Yesterday (**EP**) Columbia SEG 8174

Even More Hits From Helen: Little Miss Lonely; I Don't Care; Keep Away From Other Girls; Cry My Heart Out (**EP**) Columbia SEG8209

1963
Queen For Tonight/ Daddy Couldn't Get Me One Of Those (Columbia DB4966)

Ich war der Star heut Nacht (Queen For Tonight) Columbia, unreleased single.

Tops With Me (Number 1): Little Devil; Will Still You Love Me Tomorrow; Because They're Young; The Day The Rains Came (**EP**) Columbia SEG8229

Schlafen kann ich nie (I cried myself to sleep last night)/ Glaube mich Jonny (Columbia C22588)

Tops With Me (Number 2): Are You Lonesome Tonight; A Teenager In Love; Lipstick On Your Collar; Beyond The Sea (**EP**) Columbia SEG 7891

Mon reve est cassée (The Party's Over) Sung in French. Released on a charity LP, *Ca C'est Paris!*

Woe Is Me/ I Walked Right In
Columbia DB7206 Not Responsible/ No Trespassing
Columbia DB7072 (#1, Australia)

Look Who It Is/ Walking In My Dreams (Columbia DB7130)

1964
Fever/ Ole Father Time (Columbia DB7190)

Immer die Boys/ Warum garade ich (Columbia C22845)

Look Over Your Shoulder/ You Won't Come Home (Columbia DB7266)

Shop Around/ He Knows How To Love Me (Columbia DB7340)

I Wish I'd Never Loved You/ I Was Only Kidding (Columbia DB7395)

1965
Tomorrow Is Another Day/ It's So Funny I Could Cry (Columbia DB7517)

Sag, dass es schon ist/ Rote Rosen und Vergissmeinnicht Columbia C22997

Here In Your Arms/ Only Once (Columbia DB7587)

Something Wonderful/ Just A Line (Columbia DB7690)

1966
Forget About The Bad Things/ Wait A Little Longer (Columbia DB7810)

Ich such mir meinen Brautigam allein aus/ Der Weg zu deinem Hersen (original German composition) Columbia C23208

You've Guessed/ Take Me For A While
Pye DV14936 German release

In My Calendar/ Empty House (Columbia DB8073)

1970 (recorded 1969)
Das ist nicht die feine englische Art/ Take Down A Note Miss Smith (Columbia DV11005)

Immer Die Boys: Frag mich nicht warum; Komm' sie wieder gut; Den ton Kenn' ich schon; Gestern Nachmittag; Ich war der star heute nacht; Glaube mir Jonny; Schafen kann ich nie; Warum geread ich; Immer die Boys; Rote Rosen und Vergissmennicht; Sag' Dass es schon ist; Ich such mir meienen Brautgam alleine aus; Ein weg zu deinem Herzen; Das ist nicht die feine englische art; Walkin' Back To Happiness; Don't Treat Me Like A Child; Tout ce qu'il voudra; J'ai tant de remords; Parlons d'amour; Sans penser rien
(**LP**) BCD15509 (recorded 1961-9, release 1990)

Cilla Black

She was the only important female singer to emerge from the "Mersey Sound" explosion of the early 1960s. Indeed, along with her friends The Beatles she was almost entirely responsible for putting Liverpool on the musical map. Possessed of few airs and graces, proud of her roots, as the archetypal girl-next-door wearing neither garish clothes nor heavy make-up, she captured the hearts of the British working classes and in seven years sold more records in Britain than any contemporary. Of the seven singers in this series she remains the only one never to have been involved in a broken relationship or scandal. Her speciality was melancholy and explosive Continental ballads, in which field, even more so than Dusty Springfield, she remains unrivalled. Her readings of "You're My World", "Don't Answer Me", and "Love's Just A Broken Heart" are amongst the finest works to have ever graced the British hit-parade.

Cilla's vocal talents, whilst exceptional in this field were however almost one dimensional. When she attempted Motown, or middle-of-the-road, the result was frequently disastrous, what one imagines would be the equivalent of Maria Callas attempting a Sex Pistols cover.

Then, seemingly overnight, the hit records stopped and television took over: Cilla became the ultimate chat-show guest-turned-presenter, hosting national institutions such as *Surprise, Surprise!* And *Blind Date*, and in doing so acquiring a mixed reputation.

For her millions of fans, who supported her through her triumphs and her greatest tragedies, Cilla could do no wrong. She was and always would be one of them, a true daughter of the people. For her detractors she was variously described as "tetchy", "difficult", and even "obnoxious". This certainly never came across on the screen. Without having known her, and aside from assessing her memoirs and numerous interviews, it is not possible to form any opinion other than about her music and wonder what would have happened, had she not changed tactics and given up her brilliant singing career. One assumes that, with her innate wit and effervescent personality, the sky would have been her limit. Proof of this came when, in 1993 and celebrating her thirty years in show business, she released her fabulous *Through The Years* album...and fifteen years later when, at sixty-four, she packed out the Liverpool Empire to its rafters as the Fairy Godmother in *Cinderella*, performing songs which had been associated with her for five decades with a voice which was warmer and more powerful than ever.

One: Muse of The Mersey

She was born Priscilla Maria Veronica White at Liverpool's Stanley Street Hospital on 27 May 1943, and though her parents were no less devout Catholics than those of Dusty, her upbringing could not have been further removed hers. Liverpool, in a precarious position with its direct shipping links to the United States, had suffered badly during the Blitz. Between 1940 and 1942, the Germans had launched over eighty air-raids, causing widespread structural damage and over 4,000 fatalities. Communities were more often than not close to the bread-line, but helped each other out—unless one happened to be "Left Footers" (Catholic) and the other "Proddy Dogs" (Protestants). The Whites lived in a two-storey rented flat above a barber's shop at 380 Scotland Road. There were no modern amenities—if one wanted to take a bath, one had to drag the old tin tub in front of the fire and fill it from the copper boiler, or visit the local swimming baths once a week when gratis showers were on offer. Cilla's Irish father, John, like most of his relatives and those before them worked at the local docks: her half-Welsh mother, Priscilla Sr., nine years John's junior, ran a market stall selling second-hand clothes. As with most working-class households, however, John ruled the roost—shyly but fairly it would appear—his only cast iron rule being that the entire family attend Mass each Sunday, something he himself did not always put into practice. It was also a happy household: besides young Cilla there were elder brothers George and John, and a third brother, Allan, came along in 1948—actually a cousin which the Whites legally adopted.

School for the White children was St Anthony's, a Catholic environment which taught boys and girls together, until the age of eleven whence the sexes were segregated and strictly monitored. Cilla excelled in English and most sports, and later said that her schooldays had been amongst the happiest of her life. She also confessed to having been a tomboy and prankster, frequently getting into scrapes. In her memoirs she admits to hitching rides on the tail-plates of lorries, and "borrowing" babies left outside in their prams—a practice in these days of community spirit when neighbours trusted each other enough to leave their doors unlocked, and where no one seemed to mind so long as the child was returned after its impromptu preamble.

"I was pretty spoilt, being the only girl," she recalled, "An absolute cow if I didn't get my own way, and always an attention seeker."

Like Dusty, Cilla hated her natural (in her case mousey) hair colour and at thirteen tried to dye it auburn—leaving the paste on for too long and ending up bright red. Another catastrophe ensued, when she broke hernose during a playground escapade. In the era before rhinoplasty, it would take her years to get it fixed.

The Whites were also a musical family, in a more down to earth sense than the O'Briens—family singsongs at the local pub followed by at-home knees-ups with one of the neighbours playing the upright piano, John White on the mouth organ, Cilla Sr. impersonating "She Knows You Know!" comedienne Hylda Baker, and young Cilla singing just about everything. Her first idol was child singer Frankie Lymon, who with The Teenagers in 1956 had a big hit with "Why Do Fools Fall In Love?". Though immensely popular then, once Lymon's voice broke it would be all downhill—he died of a heroin overdose in 1968, aged just twenty-five. Cilla would drive everyone mad singing not only this but the flipside, "I'm Not A Juvenile Delinquent". She was also a fan of Frankie Vaughan, Ella Fitzgerald, Nat

King Cole, and The Platters. Finding the right acoustics was also vitally important for the budding *chanteuse*, who confessed to breaking into local factories at night not to steal, but to sing with the right echo! Like Dusty, she would grab a hairbrush and sing in front of the mirror—bringing complaints from her father, anxious to sleep in the next room after working the night shift.

Cilla's aspirations of becoming a famous singer did not diminish when she left school in July 1958. In the September, whilst confidentially waiting for this to happen, she enrolled on a secretarial course at Anfield College, and after passing her shorthand exam worked as a filing clerk with British Insular Calendar Cables. It was a boring job, but had its advantages. At lunchtimes she and her best friend Pat Davies took their sandwiches to the Cavern—and it was here that her dream started to come true.

The Cavern was the brainchild of Alan Sytner (1935-2006), an acknowledged Francophile who, not wishing to follow in his docker father's footsteps, had sunk his life savings into an entertainments venue extolling his two passions: jazz and skiffle. In 1955 during a trip to Paris, Sytner had stumbled upon Le Caveau des Oubliettes, the cellar-club tucked away in the rue Galande, in the city's lively Latin Quarter. Topping the bill had been jazz legends Sidney Bechet and Boris Vian. Bowled over by the place, Sytner had searched around Liverpool and found 10 Market Street, a former wartime air-raid shelter approached by eighteen steep stone steps. He had transformed this into a dimly lit, smoky and atmospheric exact replica of Les Oubliettes, and opened it to the public on 16 January 1957—the only difference between it and its Parisian counterpart being that, to save forking out for a liquor licence, this was a non-alcoholic establishment. Sytner's customers would come to the Cavern to listen to the music.

If they wanted to drink, then there was no shortage of pubs in the area where they could go instead.

For two years, Sytner had put on regular jazz and skiffle nights: a regular performer was Glaswegian skiffle king, Lonnie Donegan. This had worked well for a while, until the customers had become fed up with listening to the same sounds night after night, and the place began losing money. Sytner had sold up, and relocated to London. The new owner, Ray McFall, changed the entertainments schedule and set the stall for the future: his first Thursday evening "beat-night", which took place on 25 May 1960, two days before Cilla's 17th birthday, was headlined by local outfit Rory Storm & The Hurricanes—their drummer, Richard Starkey, would become renowned as Ringo Starr.

For Liverpool, these were exciting times, with over 300 venues, within which any of the city's 250 or so groups and solo artists could promote their budding talents, though at the time few would have predicted which of these would succeed and which would fade into obscurity. Eventually, The Merseybeats, The Foremost, The Searchers, The Swinging Blue Jeans, Gerry & The Pacemakers, and Billy J Kramer & The Dakotas would become household names. And, ruling the roost would be The Beatles. Inspired by Lonnie Donegan, John Lennon had formed The Quarrymen in March 1957: Paul McCartney joined the outfit a few months later, George Harrison in the spring of 1958, and bassist Stuart Sutcliffe in 1960. The group had gone through a succession of drummers, including Pete Best, before leaving England to play in the clubs around Hamburg's Reeperbahn red-light district. In 1962, Best would be replaced by Ringo Starr, and that same year Sutcliffe died suddenly of a brain haemorrhage, aged just twenty-one. The group's lunchtime debut at the Cavern took place on 21 February 1961, between overseas trips and between now and August 1963, they would notch up some 300 performances here.

Naturally friendly and gregarious, Cilla soon fell in with the Cavern's management, who for the not to be sniffed at sum of five shillings a day employed her to work her lunch hour: washing up, waiting on tables and collecting pots, and sometimes looking after the cloakroom. Her visits to the club were extended to the evenings and enabled her to get to know the artistes. And when these discovered that she could sing, the inevitable happened—they asked her to join them on the stage. Wearing a trademark black skirt and cardigan, she was good, and knew it.

Cilla's biographer, Douglas Thompson, quotes her as saying in 1991, "I know I would have always been a star anyway....My father adored me, I was the apple of his eye, and, I thought: if I'm the apple of his eye, why can't I be the apple of everybody's eye? It was no great shock to me that I had Number One records."

Though a friend of The Beatles, "Swinging Cilla", as she was billed, never got around to performing with them: this honour went to Kingsize Taylor & The Dominoes, The Big Three, and Rory Storm & The Hurricanes, none of whom despite their talent and versatility achieved much in the way of commercial success. Though she denies this in her memoirs, most authorities agree that Teddy Taylor was her first serious boyfriend—a butcher's apprentice, he stood 6 feet 5 inches in his stocking feet, and tipped the scales at a formidable 300 pounds. The group's signature tune was "Never In A Million Years", while Cilla's "showstoppers" included Ray Charles' "Unchain My Heart" and Peggy Lee's "Fever". She made her Cavern debut with The Dominoes in January 1961 and stayed with them, off-and-on, for almost a year until like The Beatles they jumped on to the Hamburg bandwagon. The Big Three had been formed (as The Casanovas) by Maltese-born vocalist-drummer Johnny Hutchinson, and for a while rivalled The Beatles—of whom Hutchinson famously quipped at the time, "They're not worth a carrot!" Their most requested songs were Ray Charles' "What'd I Say", and "Zip A Dee Doo Dah", which are included in their classic but elusive EP, *Live At The Cavern* (Decca DFE 8552), recorded in 1964 shortly before they disbanded.

Rory Storm (Alan Caldwell, 1939-72) was a tall, good looking all-round sportsman known to have had a crush on Billy Fury. When Fury's manager, Larry Parnes, offered Storm an audition he turned up at the event not because he wanted to work for Parnes, who was not averse to seducing many of his discoveries but because he knew Fury would be there. Whether they had an actual relationship is not known, but possible. A bad-tempered exhibitionist with a closeted gay following, Storm risked ridicule by appearing on stage in lavender, powder-blue or shocking-pink suits: looking more than slightly deranged, after an otherwise excellent set he would stride up the footlights and perform a novelty number, "Lend Me Your Comb", whilst running a giant comb through his thick blond locks. He and The Hurricanes had one minor hit, "I Want To Be In America", from *West Side Story*. Cilla was so close to Storm that she joined other camp-followers who travelled to the Butlins Holiday Camp, Pwllheli, to watch him perform. She blended in so well with The Hurricanes that for a time Storm considered hiring her as a permanent member. Sadly, his career would peter out. On 28 September 1972, one week after his 33rd birthday, he died following an accidental overdose of sleeping pills which reacted to medication he was taking for a chest infection. His mother, who found his body, committed suicide the same day and was discovered lying on the bed next to him. The following year, Billy Fury played him—as Tempest Storm—in the film, *That'll Be The Day*, and some years later a musical portrait, *A Need For Heroes*, opened in Liverpool.

Billy Fury occasionally played a set at the Cavern, as did Johnny Kidd & The Pirates. John Lennon, Paul McCartney and Pete Best also dropped in when they were in town. Cilla and the Cavern crowd also frequented the exceedingly noisy Iron Door, on Temple Street where it was fashionable for the kids to dress in black, like beatniks—or the Zodiac, where Cilla waitressed some evenings. There was also the Casbah Club, founded in 1959 by Pete Best's mother, Mona in the basement of her rambling Victorian house. These were the days when young women could go out alone, and not be pestered for sex by the boys they hung around with, therefore Cilla's parents were never worried if she stayed out late, well aware that as a decent Catholic girl she could be trusted.

The legend dictates that Cilla's big break occurred not at the Cavern, but at the Iron Door in November 1961 when accompanied by Lennon, McCartney, Best and George Harrison she wowed the crowd with George Gershwin's "Summertime". By this time, she had ended her courtship with Teddy Taylor, and was going out with the man who would become the great love of her life—Bobby Willis. The two met at the Zodiac, when Bobby was sporting a tan after a recent holiday in Spain, and with his sun-bleached hair she had mistaken him for a Swedish sailor!

"The last thing on my mind was romance," she recalled, "And I certainly wasn't looking for the kind of trouble that came with the 'one enchanted evening' scenario, but certain guys were always worth a few chat-up lines, especially if they looked as if they were in the money and good for a soft touch!"

Cilla was 17, and Bobby spun her a yarn that he was 21,

and that his family owned a bakery—he was just 19, and worked in the confectionary department at Woolworths! Home was a modest terraced house in Anfield—Cilla later remarked that it was the kind of home where the front room was used only for special occasions and funerals.

Reading her memoirs, *What's It All About?*, sparkling and refreshing in their honesty, though she is fond of the occasional "tall tale", one almost believes Cilla's feeble admission that she was not looking for marriage—just a nice "fella" to take her out and treat her to a little fun, her excuse being that all that really mattered was launching her career. If any show business union appears to have been made in heaven, theirs does. Like many women of her generation and background, Cilla had been raised to acknowledge the man as boss in any relationship, and Bobby gives every impression of being just that, albeit gently remonstrative and quietly possessive, not overtly romantic (her own admission), but above all putting the welfare of his wife and family first. In an environment not renowned for the longevity of its marriages, the two would remain inseparable for the rest of Bobby's life, a veritable inspiration to their colleagues and peers.

And if Bobby Willis provided Cilla with her anchor, the next man to enter her life would become her Svengali. Brian Epstein had been born into a well-to-do Jewish family in Liverpool's Rodney Street in September 1934. Boarding school educated, sophisticated, and always impeccably dressed, his ambition had been to become a dress designer, but his father had made him work in the family's department store, NEMS. In 1951, aged 17, he had been drafted into the Royal Army Service Corps and posted to the Albany Street Barracks, near London's Regent's Park. Here, he commissioned a Saville Row tailor to make him an officer's uniform—which he wore while cruising for gay sex, his favourites being the "Dilly Boys" who plied their trade around the Piccadilly area. His big mistake wearing it during a visit to the Army & Navy Club. Apprehended by the Military Police he evaded court-marshal only by agreeing to see an Army psychiatrist with a view to curing him of his "affliction". Subsequently, he was discharged from the Army as "emotionally and mentally unstable", for no other reason than he was attracted to me, pre-1967 when homosexuality was illegal in Britain, even between consenting adults. Epstein had next enrolled with RADA, where he studied with Albert Finney and Susanna York. Whilst here he developed a taste for cottaging: on one occasion the man he had sex with stole his wallet, passport, and birth certificate. Eventually, he was arrested by a police *agent provocateur*. This incident saw him dropping out of acting, and returning to Liverpool, where his father put him in charge of the record department at NEMS, one of the biggest in Northern England—and one of those long-gone delightful institutions where one could stand in plywood booths and listen to the latest hits of the day before buying them. With a natural flair for business, Epstein had opened a second store on Whitechapel.

According to the legend, a man named Raymond Jones had walked into NEMS on 28 October 1961 and asked for a copy of The Beatles' "My Bonnie" which they had recorded as Tony Sheridan & The Beat Brothers, in Germany. Epstein, curious, had subsequently gone to see them at the Cavern on 9 November. This is untrue. Epstein was already contributing a column to *Mersey Beat* magazine—founded by Bill Harry, a friend of John Lennon from his Liverpool Art College days—and had his finger firmly on the pulse. He also knew Bob Wooler (1926-2002), the Cavern's resident compere who had managed The Kingstrums skiffle group, and who besides deejaying here was involved in just about every aspect of the Mersey scene. As such, whatever advice he had to offer was invariably taken seriously. Wooler had just rejected an offer to manage The Beatles, assured that Epstein would do a better job. It was *he* who arranged the famous meeting at the Cavern which led to Epstein signing the group to a five-year contract on 24 January 1962. What is astonishing is that so many record companies turned them down until Parlophone—the subsidiary of EMI run by George Martin, then the producer of the Goons's radio show and often referred to as "The Fifth Beatle"—took them on. The rest, to coin an old cliché, is history. After touring with Helen Shapiro, the group recorded "Love Me Do" at Martin's Abbey Road Studios. This reached Number 17 in the charts but its successor, "Please Please Me" hit the cherished top spot. From this point the man nicknamed "Eppydemic" and his "stable of golden boys" never looked back. Over the coming months Gerry & The Pacemakers topped the charts with "How Do You Do It?", Billy J Kramer & The Dakotas had a big hit with Lennon and McCartney's "Do You Want To Know A Secret?", and The Beatles topped the charts again with "From Me To You".

Epstein's homosexuality stayed an open secret amongst those closest to him. He is alleged to have had flings with several subsequently married frontmen, including John Lennon (who claimed that Epstein's autobiography, *A Cellarfull Of Noise* should have been retitled *A Cellarfull Of Boys*) and Rory Storm—a regular drinker at Epstein's occasional hang-out, the Magic Clock, in Hood Street. He is also thought to have had an unreciprocated crush on Tommy Quickly, the insecure vocalist with The Reno Four, and one of his few failures. Matters came to a head during an incident on 18 June 1963, the occasion being Paul McCartney's twenty-first birthday. Epstein and Lennon had just returned from a holiday in Spain, and Bob Wooler loudly suggested that while there they had slept together—resulting in an irate Lennon laying into Wooler, putting him in hospital. Wooler sued him but Epstein, terrified of being outed by the press, paid Wooler £200 to keep quiet. Pete Best also claimed that Epstein had propositioned him. To cope with his "problem", Epstein took stimulants. Unable to have sex with the young men who took his fancy, he seduced them in other ways—moulding them for stardom, changing their dress and appearance, teaching them how to conduct themselves on the stage. The Beatles in particular were pretty crude when they started out at the Cavern, frequently performing with "chip butties" in their hands. Though Epstein never taught them sophistication, he taught them manners.

Because the Mersey scene was so dominated, and doubtless because of his sexual orientation, Brian Epstein (Cilla always pronounced his name *Epsteen*) showed scant interest in female entertainers—not that there were many good ones in Liverpool at this time. Cilla's main rival was Beryl Marsden (Beryl Hogg), four years her junior. At the age of fifteen, Marsden had begun singing with The Undertakers. Though their gimmick was to perform in a setting which incorporated a Wild West hearse and coffin, as musicians they were impressive. They recorded an excellent cover version of Doris Day's "Everybody Loves A Lover", and for a while were almost as popular as The Beatles and Rory Storm. When The Undertakers, Storm, and The Beatles left to perform in Hamburg, both Cilla and Marsden would have accompanied them, had they not been underage and unable to acquire work permits. Marsden became a regular at the Cavern, where she became known as Liverpool's answer to Brenda Lee. Her debut single, "I Know", was later covered by Sandie Shaw.

There has been speculation that, had John Lennon put in a good word for Marsden, and had Epstein championed her instead of Cilla, then Marsden might have ended up the major star. One doubts this. Despite its flaws in the upper range, Cilla had a far better voice and she also had the one quality that cannot be taught—an innate charisma.

Cilla's audition, which saw her accompanied by The Beatles, took place at the Majestic Cinema, in Birkenhead. She sang George Gershwin's "Summertime" in one key, while they played in another! Unimpressed, Epstein concentrated on his other acts until he happened to be in the audience at the Blue Angel Club on Seel Street. Cilla was singing with John Rubin's Jazz Band, and received a big applause for her take on Judy Garland's "You Made Me Love You", blithely unaware that Epstein was watching from the back of the auditorium.

"I watched her move, and I watched her stand," Epstein recalled in his memoirs, "And I half closed my eyes and imagined her on a vast stage with the right lighting. I was convinced she would become a wonderful artiste."

Afterwards in the dressing room, Epstein reassured Cilla that she was much better with ballads than she was with rock and roll, and promised her the contract that she should have had months ago—though nothing was signed as yet. The reason for his deliberation was Bob Wooler, also in the Blue Angel that evening. Wooler had never had anything but praise for Cilla, and well aware of her budding talent nurtured plans to manage her himself. In an attempt to dissuade Epstein from signing her, he denounced her as a "hopeless wonder". There may, however, be other reasons why Epstein hedged before taking Cilla on.

"The one thing she had in common with Dot Squires was that both were always surrounded by queens," Nicky Welsh told me. "If you saw Cilla out with a guy, no matter who he was, he'd inadvertently let the cat out of the bag. And Cilla's husband was intensely homophobic, which was confusing to say the least."

Welsh, Dorothy's and at one time Cilla's arranger, was referring to the coterie of middle-aged, over-the-top gay friends she later gathered about her—the ones she jokingly referred to by her as her "gay mafia".

She would later say of her friends' sexual preferences, "Showbusiness is one business in which we don't care what people are: there is no prejudice towards homosexuals, lesbians and colour. We are as one."

Sadly, this was not always the case. In her memoirs, ghosted at a time when she should have known better, she uses terms like "a bit of a soft quilt" and stereotypes him by writing that he was "much more at home with Judy Garland than any R and B or rock group."

Worse still, back in 1963, in an outburst which may only be categorised as "mother's-milk homophobia", she admits to responding to Epstein's offer of a contract with, "I don't know if I should, because the word's going around that you buy mohair suits for boys."

Elsewhere in her memoirs she says that, until she was twenty-two when one of her friends was gay-bashed and Bobby enlightened her on the subject (using the word "gay", not yet in everyday usage, which casts doubt on the story), she had no idea what homosexuals did in bed.

"Before that," she observed, "I'd only gleaned that some men liked to dress up in women's clothes, and that some men had no sexual interest in women's clothes, and that some men had no sexual interest in women, never got married, and remained 'confirmed bachelors'."

Was she really *so* naive? Nicky Welsh believed that Epstein had second thoughts about taking Cilla on because of such comments albeit that she was not being deliberately malicious—though in a "macho" city renowned for its (then) anti-gay attitude, he had doubtless heard worse. Even so, homophobic jibes—even in jest—cut Epstein deeply. Unable to have a steady relationship with a man of his choosing he resorted to rent boys, and to cope with the resulting depression, not to mention the fear of blackmail, he drank heavily and became addicted to drugs.

Another reason for delaying Cilla's contract rested with George Martin, who was yet to hear her. The opportunity came yet again courtesy of The Fortunes, whose last minute appearance on *Ready, Steady, Go!* left the studio with a vacant slot. Martin called Epstein, and he arranged for Cilla's trip to London—her first, which she equated to setting off for darkest Peru—for which Epstein had to obtain permission from her father, fiercely protective of his daughter's reputation. John White gave in when Bobby promised to look after her—such were his honourable intentions that there was never any question of them not sleeping in separate rooms. The couple arrived in London on 24 July, and the following day she made two test recordings for Martin, and an acetate for Dick James—he of the *Robin Hood* theme-song fame, and co-founder with Epstein of The Beatles' Northern Songs. Interestingly, at around this time James offered Bobby, himself no mean singer-songwriter, a recording contract—which he turned down declaring that "one singer in the family was enough". Clearly, Cilla had found herself a true rock.

Cilla's accompanists for the session were The Bruisers, a trio of musicians led by Les Reed, who later composed for Tom Jones and Engelbert Humperdinck. Also brought in were Gerry & The Pacemakers. The song laid down for Dick James was Peggy Lee's "Fever"—made cringeworthy by Cilla's pronouncing the words "bare" and "care" as "burr" and "curr". Next up, and only marginally better—she tends to shout rather than sing the lyrics—was Terry Thompson's "A Shot Of Rhythm And Blues", a 1962 hit for Johnny Kidd & The Pirates. Finally, there was "Shy Of Love", a fine calypso-style piece written by Bobby Willis which easily compares with some of the material which Dusty was recording at this time. It's only fault, albeit a minor one, was that like most of his compositions it was way too short.

Accustomed to performing in comfortable, intimate surrounds such as were provided by the Cavern, Cilla initially found working in the studio clinical, with no public response to confirm how well she had done, she said. Even so, she passed the audition for George Martin and on 28 August—still unrepresented—she returned to Abbey Road to record her first single for Parlophone. For obvious reasons she had wanted this to be "Shy Of Love", but Epstein and Martin decided that she would record Lennon and McCartney's "Love Of The Loved", which had been doing the rounds for a while. The group had performed it in Hamburg, and in 1962 had recorded it as part of a 15-song failed audition for Decca, whence they had given it to Beryl Marsden. Now, Epstein pressurised Lennon into giving it to Cilla, who effectively became the very first artiste to record a cover of a Beatles song. "A brassy number for a brassy voice," George Martin observed. It would be rush-released on 27 September 1963, with "Shy Of Love" on the flipside. The voice is powerful, controlled and like much of the black music then winging its way across the Atlantic there is a riveting brass interlude between the middle and final stanzas. The "thurr" and "curr" are still there, but excusable because the whole reading is so good. Only a lack of airplay prevented it from going higher than Number 35 in the charts, it was a more than impressive effort, and a sure sign of better things to come.

Two: A Dream Come True

Cilla's first professional concert appearance, once again standing in for The Foremost who were still busy with television work, took place on 30 August 1963—topping the bill were The Beatles. She recalled how John Lennon had helped her cope with her nerves, by cracking, "Go knock 'em out girl—failing that, just show 'em your knickers!" Accompanied by a country and western band, she sang the three songs she had auditioned for George Martin, but to a noisy crowd who were interested only in one thing. Beatlemania had begun, with scenes of pandemonium and hysteria the likes of which had not seen since Johnnie Ray had stormed into Britain in the 1950s. After the show, Brian Epstein finally offered her a contract, which would not become legally binding until 6 September, when on account of her being under twenty-one, it would have to be countersigned by her father. Initially, John White opposed the name Cilla Black on the document. In Northern England at this time, changing one's name unless by marriage usually meant that one was ashamed of one's family. Neither was this the first time, apparently, that Cilla had taken a prospective manager home for Sunday tea to meet parents who, if the visitor was not Catholic or Proestant or speaking with a local accent, treated him with suspicion. Epstein failed on all counts, but seems to have won John White over because, a few years earlier, he had sold the Whites their piano. The contract was duly signed.

Much has been said about how she came to be known as Cilla Black. In fact, the appellation had come from Bill Harry, writing on 6 July 1961 in the very first issue of *Mersey Beat*, having commissioned Cilla to write a short feature about her tastes in fashion and, having forgotten her surname whilst well aware that it was a colour, had accidentally called her Cilla Black! This was picked up on by Bob Wooler, writing in the magazine's 5 October 1961:

> She has a voice which is vibrant, unusual, swingy, penetrating—and controversial. You either rave over her voice or it leaves you cold. There's no compromise. Talk of her, and you find on the one hand she is self-deprecating, and on the other hand she has aspirations of combining in her voice the qualities of Ella Fitzgerald or Della Reese. At least she is setting herself high enough standards. Let no one say she is misguided in her ambitions, not in this age of four-letter words when day is night and Black is White!

The day after signing the contract, George Martin came up with the "groovy" publicity slogan, "The Girl With The Jet Black Voice, The Bird In A Beat Boy's World". Martin then set about grooming her for stardom, a process to which was applied the minimum effort. Thinking along the lines of turning her into a latter day Gracie Fields, he begged her to stay exactly as she was: inarticulate, loquacious, a little rough around the edges but decent, and unaffected, qualities which would see her becoming the nation's working class sweetheart, in direct contrast to Dusty and the slightly later Marianne Faithfull. Not long afterwards, Cilla gave up her job with Calendar Cables.

    Epstein put her to work at once, adding her to the line-up of a Gerry & The Pacemakers tour which kicked off on 4 October took in 28 cinemas and theatres up and down the country, and culminated in a concert at the Liverpool Empire. If Cilla had found working in the studio tedious, television would prove a much tetchier environment to get used to. She had coped reasonably well in the "hot seat" on *Juke Box Jury*—"doing a Lauren Bacall" by lighting up a cigarette and earning herself a ticking off from her manager who considered it common for a woman to smoke. She had also mimed "Love Of The Loved" on ITV's *Discs-a-Gogo*. A few days later, however, performing the song live on a Southampton teatime magazine, she got carried away—not knowing what to do during the brass interlude, she began dancing, and danced off camera leaving astonished viewers gaping at an empty screen! By the time she appeared on *Thank Your Lucky Stars* with Billy J Kramer, though, she was conducting herself like a hardened professional.

In December 1963, in the wake of Dusty Springfield's debut single entering the charts and the talk of her aspirations for international stardom, Brian Epstein boasted that he would make *his* new star a bigger worldwide sensation than Edith Piaf—not a sensible thing to say, considering Piaf had died only weeks before. The response from grieving Piaf fans was to send to London for copies of "Love Of The Loved" and publicly burn them outside Paris's Gare du Nord railway station. Epstein may have found this amusing, though he must have been laughing on the other side of his face when a delegation of French theatre and television executives, headed by the Olympia's Bruno Coquatrix, informed him that Cilla Black would never be invited to sing in France. As such, she remains the only major 1960s Brit Girl not to have done so. The nearest she got to France was when bandleader Aimé Barelli asked her to sing once at Le Sporting Club de Monte Carlo.

Cilla featured in *The Beatles Christmas Show*, a revue of sorts which opened at the Finsbury Park Astoria on Christmas Eve, and which saw the group on stage for just 25 minutes. Compered by Rolf Harris, the bill included The Barron Knights, The Fourmost, Billy J Kramer and Tommy

Quickly, now coming towards the end of his career—he retired the following year. Quickly's singles had all failed to chart. Drinking heavily and addicted to drugs, on stage he could be unpredictable. His big song in the show was Lennon and McCartney's "Tip Of The Tongue", which he frequently messed up—not that anyone noticed, or even heard what was being sung by *anyone* for the constant din coming from the screaming fans who had snapped up the 85,000 tickets for the 28 performances in just two days. These blocked all the streets surrounding the theatre. When Cilla and the other acts balked at having to spend Christmas away from their families, Epstein—ensconced in his new London office—personally forked out £400 and chartered a Viking aircraft to return them to Liverpool, the first time most of them had flown.

The Beatles Christmas Show closed on 11 January 1964, to the merciful relief of anyone living close to the Astoria!
The previous afternoon, Cilla had entered the Abbey Road Studios to record her second single, Dionne Warwick's (but first performed by Marlene Dietrich) "Anyone Who Had A Heart", originally earmarked for Shirley Bassey, and the song which would earn her Warwick's eternal emnity. Some years later, Cilla would say on national television (*Cilla*, the documentary) in such a way that it was hard to tell if she joking or not, "Dionne, the cow that she is....Ha, ha! No, I say that because we had this sort of love-hate relationship, I think. I love her as much as she hates me!", and leave the quote unfinished. Warwick's version of the song was already out in America on the Spector label, but there was a delay with its overseas release owing to a licensing hitch between the company and Pye Records. George Martin took advantage of this and, without even contacting Bacharach and David, deliberately gazumped Warwick by releasing Cilla's recording on 31 January, with

Bobby's "Just For You" on the flipside. This song perfectly sums up the couple's devotion to each other—"I'm content with just one boy to last me the rest of my days,"—which is exactly how things would turn out.

Whereas Dionne Warwick's interpretation of "Anyone Who Has A Heart" is pedestrian, robotically delivered and almost completely devoid of feeling, Cilla put her very heart and soul into her reading, ably accompanied by future *Top Of The Pops* bandleader-arranger Johnny Pearson. She was suitably rewarded by having it shoot to the top of the UK charts—the first time a female singer had done this since Helen Shapiro, in 1961—where it remained for three weeks. Though Dusty's version may have been technically superior, it is Cilla's powerhouse performance we will always remember. The record went silver, then gold, selling 850,000 copies by the end of the summer. Indeed, until Alexandra Burke's 2008 cover of Leonard Cohen's and Jeff Buckley's "Hallelujah" (by which time sales were being augmented by downloads) it remained the top-selling single by a British female artiste. Cilla beat all of her Merseyside contemporaries—*and* The Rolling Stones—to top the *New Musical Express*'s "All British Top Ten In History" poll, collecting her award at Wembley on 26 April.

In the meantime, Cilla embarked on a hectic, 36-date tour with Billy J Kramer, The Swinging Blue Jeans, Tommy Quickly and Gene Pitney, along with a nine-date stint at Blackpool's Queen's Theatre. She experienced for the first time the inconvenience of zigzagging up and down the country in a communal tour bus. "Totally unsexy," she recalled, "Farts, belches, five o'clock shadows, smelly socks and vests, and Bobby was as bad as the rest of them." Such comments may give the impression that Cilla was "one of the gang", but the phase was short-lived as success soon went to her head. From now on, only the very best would do: the best clothes, restaurants and cars. After her Mary Quant black plastic mackintosh was ripped by mobbing fans, she opted for the "Hollywood" look—mink coats, jewels. She bought a Jag, decided that this did not quite befit her station, and only days later bought a Bentley because Brian Epstein had one.

"In her eyes, he was a ten-percenter, whilst she was the star," future arranger Nicky Welsh said, "So why should he drive a more expensive motor than her?"

In every show, "Anyone Who Had A Heart" received such wild applause that Cilla sometimes sang it again. Dionne Warwick was furious that someone had stolen what she regarded her signature tune, denouncing Cilla as "dreadful", and "a little English upstart" whilst knowing absolutely nothing about her. In May 1997, the two clashed in the US television special, *The Great Performances: Burt Bacharach*, when Warwick declared that Cilla had copied her performance so verbatim that, had *she* coughed in the middle of the song or the organist played just one note out of key, Cilla would have done exactly the same. Cilla only had a cameo in the production, but she managed to get her point across. "It was Number One," she piped, "Dionne was dead choked, and she's never forgiven me to this day!"

In fact, under the terms laid down by Burt Bacharach's music publisher, changing the song's arrangement was prohibited—and the same applied to its successor, which Cilla recorded after just two takes on 3 April. Unlike others she did not place Bacharach on a pedestal, believing that there were many other good composers around—besides which, *she* had The Beatles on her side.

When asked by the *New Musical Express* what her next record would be, she had enthused, "It'll have to be upbeat. Real *wild* R & B if I can get away with it. And I'd like to do calypso and blues. Oh, I'd love to all kind of way out stuff if they'll let me!"

Some years later in the television documentary, *Cilla*, Ringo Starr half-joked that, had she gone down this particular road, her career would have been over inside three weeks! Calypso, George Martin now told her, was more Sandie Shaw's style, and Dusty held the monopoly on rhythm and blues. Therefore she left the choice to Brian Epstein, who searched towards Europe for the song which, he hoped, would prove just as successful as the last.

"Il mio mondo" had been a massive hit in Italy for singer-songwriter Umberto Bindi (1932-2002), whose "Di fronte all'amore" had been adapted for Dusty Springfield. Bindi, who had much in common with Epstein in that he was desperate to hide his homosexuality from the world (when the news eventually broke, it ended his career) had written the song with regular partner Gino Paoli. Adapted into English by Carl Sigman—famed for working his magic on Continental favourites (most recently "What Now My Love?"), it became "You're My World" and was released on 1 May. From its short-notes violin introduction and Cilla's intimate, close to the mike opening stanza to its robust climax, it is a gem with which she excels, without any doubt setting a precedent resulting in her Italian songs being the finest she ever performed. Its only fault occurs when she pronounces the line, "With your hand resting on mine,"—the "hand" is overtly nasal, and would have benefitted a retake. Few were surprised when it shot to the top of the charts where it remained for five weeks. As such, she had become the first British female singer to have had two Number Ones. The B-side, "Suffer Now I Must", was again penned by Bobby. The record was also a hit in America—her first and last. Elvis Presley even considered a cover version, but deciding he would never compete with

Cilla, settled for having a copy of her record on his jukebox at Graceland. Not to be outdone, Dionne Warwick put out a rival version which flopped majestically.

In London, on 27 May, Cilla celebrated her twenty-first birthday. Following an appearance on *Ready, Steady, Go!* she had become close friends with Cathy McGowan: the two could sometimes be seen shopping around King's Road and Carnaby Street. McGowan's then hairdresser boyfriend gave her a new, "geometric bob" look which suited her sharp, angular features. Though she was a typical "dolly bird" who favoured the latest Mary Quant fashions, when on stage belting out her big ballads, she preferred wearing long dresses. Her new look caught the attention of Val Parnell, who took advantage of the "You're My World" fever and offered her a two weeks stint in his latest revue at the Palladium: *Startime* was headlined by Tommy Cooper, Frankie Vaughan, and comedienne Audrey Jeans. Though she only had three songs, such was her popularity that she was asked to stay on—with the twice-nightly shows and matinees, by the end of the year she would notch up over 300 performances.

Startime also witnessed the birth of Cilla Black the prima donna, a trait which would intensify over the years. Firstly, she refused to take curtain calls during the revue's finale, declaring that she had done her bit and that she had no intention of hanging around just to bow with the rest of the cast. She soon changed her mind when the management threatened to fire her for not doing so. Next, tired of her shabby dressing room, she asked for it to be redecorated—a request which was granted, setting a precedent for tougher demands later in her career. Her insistence that her group, Sounds Incorporated, should back her because she disliked performing with the resident orchestra backfired. Val Parnell was an exceedingly tetchy man and some traditions, such this and the theatres famous revolving stage, would never change.

On 5 July, Cilla took a break from *Startime* to return to Liverpool, where she had been given a cameo in *Ferry Cross The Mersey*, an unbelievably dire exercise in hokum centered around Gerry & The Pacemakers. Shot locally, it tells the story of a bunch or art students (Gerry Marsden and his musicians) who have to recover their instruments when these are accidentally dispatched to the airport. They then go on to win a talent contest, and of course hit the big time. Though Marsden's title-track remains iconic, an anthem to the city and its river, Cilla's segment is the film's only redeeming feature. Shot at the Locarno Ballroom, on stage and at times in extreme close-up, she performs Bobby's most endearing song, "Is It Love?" Brian Epstein, who part produced the film, and writer Tony *(Coronation Street)* Warren were hoping for big things, but it flopped and so far as is known has never been shown on television or released on video. Even the tagline is naff: "The Big Beat Is Back With The Excitingest New Pacemaking Pack!" One may only wonder what acknowledged character actors Derek Guyler and Mona Washbourne were thinking about when they signed up to appear in it.

Cilla's follow-up to "You're My World" was a Lennon and McCartney classic, "It's For You" backed with Bobby's "He Won't Ask Me". Written in the style of a waltz, her timing is spot on in an unusual piece which incorporates a large number of key and tempo changes which most non-classical singers would have found impossible to handle. Paul McCartney suitably demonstrates this, and how *not* to sing it, with the demo he recorded shortly before Cilla's version was released on 31 July. Her arrangement is by Johnny Spence, who in just over two minutes leads her through a dichotomy of vocal pyrotechnics—ballad, R & B, jazz, soul—before having her jump a whole octave to Top C! John Lennon and Paul McCartney were present when she performed it at Granada Studios, where the producer put her into the shortest dress imaginable and coaxed her into mounting a scaffold, mindless of her fear of heights. Then on she crossed a gangplank while the pair gaped up at her—"copping an eyeful", Lennon later said, whilst the structure shook on account of the quartet of musclebound dancers swinging from it and executing somersaults in tune to the music. The record reached Number 7 in the charts, disappointing her, she said, because she had been hoping it would complete a hat-trick of Number Ones.

On 8 November, Cilla was an eleventh hour addition to that year's *Royal Variety Performance*, and may not have known that Brian Epstein had worked behind the scenes to get her on the bill, at Dusty Springfied's expense.

"Well, she was already there and earning a lot of money for the theatre, and you've already signed Tommy Cooper," Epstein is quoted as saying to Bernard Delfont.

As usual it was an impressive line-up which included Kathy Kirby, Tommy Cooper and Lena Horne. Topping the bill was Gracie Fields, who took an instant dislike to Cilla, who performed "You're My World".

"She was too full of herself," Gracie told her friend Mary Whipp, "She thought she was better than everybody else there. I think she expected to be on stage all night instead of singing just one song. And when they introduced her to the Queen, would she heckers like stop talking. You could see that Her Majesty was getting annoyed and couldn't move along the line-up fast enough!"

For Cilla's next single, Brian Epstein and George Martin had done another spot of gazumping. The Righteous Brothers had recently topped the US charts with Barry Mann, Cynthia Weill and Phil Spector's "You've Lost That

Loving Feeling", resplendent with Spector's infamous Wall of Sound technique. What no one had asked was, who were "brothers" Bill Medley and Bobby Hatfield expressing their feelings of dispondence to—a woman they had shared, or each other? As such it had become a favourite with San Francisco's gay community. Cilla recorded her version in December 1964: much better suited to a solo performer, it was released on 5 February 1965, only days after The Righteous Brother's original, giving them the slight edge over airplay. Even so, whilst their record shot to the top of the UK charts, Cilla's peaked at Number Two—having turned base metal into pure gold, had she sold just a few hundred copies more that first week, she would have beat them to the top spot. In some quarters, there was not unexpected bitterness, though not from the songwriters. The Rolling Stones' manager, Andrew Oldham, was incensed by Cilla's technically superior version of the song, and placed an ad in *Melody Maker*, proclaiming that The Righteous Brothers' recording was the best record ever made—not that this made any difference to sales of the rival version. For the first time in chart history, the same song held the Number One and Two spots. This would happen only twice more—in 1967 with "This Is My Song" (Petula Clark, Harry Secombe) and with "Hallelujah" in 2008 (Alexandra Burke, Jeff Buckley). Cilla's recording reached Number Two in the Australian charts, resulting in a flood of offers for her to tour there.

In the meantime, coinciding with a three-week tour with American singer P J Proby—he of the splitting trousers fame and whose on-stage antics saw him replaced by Tom Jones halfway through the run—Cilla released her debut album. With *Cilla*, George Martin had assembled a "white British soul" package which he hoped would help her crack the US market—his theory being that, if Dusty could do it, so could his girl. What Martin had not reckoned with was the distinctive differences between their voices. Whereas Dusty produced a mellow sound, even when singing in the upper register, much of the time whilst attempting these American songs, Cilla frequently sets one's teeth on edge. Even so, the album has its moments, the good ones just about outweighing the bad, and the fans liked it, sending it to Number 5 in the charts.

The album It opens with "Goin' Out Of My Head", a recent hit for Little Anthony & The Imperials which starts off well enough, but becomes overbearing towards the end. Next up is the positively horrendous "Baby It's You", a hit for both The Shirelles and The Beatles—the only Bacharach-David song the group covered. "Dancing In The Street" is a revelation, proving that, had Martin allowed her to record a few more items of this calibre, Cilla would have had a classic album to assign to pop history. Then it is back to the mediocre with Jerome Kern's "Old Man River": Johnny Spence's big band arrangement works to a degree, until Cilla murders the whole thing with her "Bronx-honk" embellishments.

Side Two of *Cilla* opens with Luigi Coppola's "Little Voice"—as "Uno di voi" a recent hit for 17-year-old Gigliola Cinquetti, who had won Eurovision Song the previous year. Cilla's interpretation is amazing. The song starts off like "You're My World", the voice breathy and warm, gradually building up to a stupendous crescendo which sends shivers down the spine. Italian songs would become Cilla's speciality, for which she was unequalled. A sensible move would have been to release this as a single: instead, Parlophone leased it out to Capitol for the flipside of Bobby's "Is It Love?", put out in America ahead of her forthcoming tour. Almost as good is Clive Westlake and Kenny Lynch's "I'm Not Alone Anymore", turned down by

Dusty, and a difficult piece with tricky key changes. Again, Cilla would excel more than any Sixties contemporary when it came to complex arrangements. Then it is back to the "iffy" with The Small Faces honky-tonk "Whatcha Gonna Do About It?" Next comes Victor Young's "Love Letters", written in 1945 for Dick Haymes, though the best-known version was that by Ketty Lester in 1962. Here, Cilla harmonises well with Sounds Incorporated. And after Bacharach and David's "This Empty Place"—well, there had to be at least one Dionne Warwick song to show her how it should be done!—the album rounds of with Cole Porter's "You'd Be So Nice To Come To", of which the least said the better. A mixed bag, no mistake!

In the middle of March, Cilla and Bobby flew to Sydney for a brief tour of Australia and New Zealand. Brian Epstein had given strict instructions that their romance be kept under wraps. In the Sixties, it was not considered au fait for a male pop singer to let on that he was married or amorously involved, the theory being that if he was "taken" the girls would stop swooning and buying his records. This did not apply if he was gay, in which case "lavender" relationships were essential. The same principle did not apply to female stars, but having had no experience in this field other than with Cilla, Epstein was taking no chances. When invited to that year's Royal Film Performance, *Lord Jim*, Epstein himself had been her "date" for the evening. Even in England, where they were hardly ever apart, Bobby was still officially listed as her road manager. When Australian reporters began speculating about a relationship between Cilla and her support act, "Venus In Blue Jeans" singer Mark Wynter, the truth emerged—and of course made not one jot of difference—though initially, fearing a ticking off from Epstein, she denied that she and Bobby were close. Epstein, adept when it came to organising tours on home soil, was not so good at arranging things overseas, and had booked the pair into the most inappropriate venues. These included a boxing stadium in Sydney which reeked of sweat, and a Perth swimming pool where the show played, next to the water while the place was still open for business! In Darwin, a large proportion of the audience left the outdoor theatre when attacked by a plague of flying cockroaches!

No sooner had Cilla arrived back in London than George Martin had her in the studio again. The success of *Cilla* and the critical singling out of "Dancing In The Street" and "Every Little Bit Hurts" had given him the idea to package her like Dusty in preparation for her visit to the United States, only days away. By and large, this was a mistake. She had recorded "Some Things You Never Get Used To", a big hit for Irma Thomas, before leaving for Australia, and during her absence Martin had been on the lookout for other black music to enhance her repertoire. "Poor Boy", which he wanted to put out as a single but one, was one of her best recordings that year. "Shotgun" was a cover of Junior Walker's signature tune. Cilla's reading has a nice saxophone introduction, but immediately becomes dreadful the moment she comes in, positively screeching as opposed to singing the lyrics. There seems little doubt that, had she attempted to sing this in America, on account of Walker's reverence she might have experienced a frosty reception. "The Cherry Song" and "Please Don't Ask Me To Love You", from the same session are almost as bad. By contrast, Cilla is in sparkling form in "Anytime You Need Me", a superb soul classic arranged by Johnny Spence—it is the ear-shattering wailing Sounds Incorporated which lets her down. Thankfully, with the exception of "Poor Boy" these songs assigned to the EMI vaults, where they would remain for many years.

On 2 April, Cilla flew to New York where Brian Epstein had secured her a three-week engagement at the Plaza Hotel's Persian Room. On 5 April she appeared on Ed Sullivan's top-rating *Toast Of The Town*, where she sang "Dancing In The Street" and "You're My World"—the first song, a triumph of mind over matter, resulted in her being filmed from the waist upwards not because she was emulating Elvis Presley's controversial early appearances on Sullivan's show, but because one of Kublers' Chimps, also in the show, waddled on to the stage and began humping her leg! Neither did Sullivan inspire confidence by introducing her as "a girl singer from Wales"!

The next evening, she returned to the studio to tape two more segments for Sullivan, which were completed once the regular show had aired. These were to be incorporated into a Liverpool Special headlined by The Beatles—their segments would be taped on 14 August and the show broadcast on 12 September. With a new, fluffed out hairdo she sang "Going Out Of My Head", and an up-tempo "September In The Rain"—which saw her encouraging the frosty audience by yelling, "Come on!", whence they began clapping along. On *Shindig*, hosted by Jimmy O'Neil, she received a standing ovation for Randy Newman's superb "I've Been Wrong Before". The Persian Room she did not like, as it was an establishment which catered for wealthy businessmen who looked down their noses at her because her publicity stated she came from a working-class background. Peggy Lee and Eartha Kitt had performed here and hated the place. Cilla made the big mistake of thinking that she was in some cosy cabaret back home, instead of a room full of snobs. Her first show comprised the twelve songs from the new album, along with her UK hits—only "You're My World" earned a decent applause. Had Epstein organised an American representative to advise her what to sing in an attempt to please these people, things might have turned out differently. Instead, it was a case of trial and error—of dropping any songs which had not gone down well and replacing them with show tunes and standards. Unfortunately, Cilla did not strike this happy medium until it was too late, when she was into her final week.

Cilla would never make it big in America. Maybe she was too quintessentially English to even care: Britain had made her, the British public had taken her to their insular hearts without expecting her to change a single fibre of her persona. Maybe, after her experiences in the Persian Room, Cilla did not *want* to take any more risks—it being a case of, "Better the devil you know." She also had a distinct advantage over her contemporaries in that she was a natural raconteur-comedienne with a ready wit and innate sense of timing. These were the qualities which, long after her pop days were over, endeared her to millions. It mattered little what the critics thought, the ones who labelled her "tetchy". So far as the fans were concerned, she could do no wrong. And in her eyes, aside from her family, the fans' opinions were all that mattered. Dusty was mysterious. Marianne was aloof. One cannot imagine them, for example, opening up on chat shows, or being invited to switch on the Blackpool illuminations. Though she enjoyed enormous chart success—selling more records than any of her Brit Girls rivals—Cilla was essentially a performance artiste.

Having decided that Cilla's forte was ballads, George Martin got her to record "I've Been Wrong Before" (c/w Bobby's "I Don't Want To Know"), a mature piece which she handles well—it's only problem being that, at just two minutes, it is way too short. Released in April, it stalled at Number 17 in the charts. Even so, Randy Newman, yet to begin recording his own material, is on record as saying that it was his favourite cover of all his songs. Interestingly, he made the same comment about the versions by Peggy Lee and Dusty Springfield.

By now, Cilla had left Liverpool and she and Bobby were living together in London, albeit discreetly. They had bought a cottage in Prince Albert Terrace Mews, near Regent's Park—a stop-gap, she said, until they could find somewhere more grand. She had also bought a house just outside Liverpool for her parents. At the end of the year she played the lead in *Little Red Riding Hood*, opposite Jon Pertwee, at the Wimbledon Theatre. The six-week run was a sell-out. During rehearsals, she later confessed, a friend persuaded her to smoke a joint—an experience which made her so ill, she vowed never to touch the stuff again.

There are simply not enough superlatives in the English language to describe Cilla's next single, "Love's Just A Broken Heart", which kick-started 1966 and which peaked at Number 5 in the charts. The song had been around for a few years. Michele Vendome had written "L'amour est ce qu'il est" for Edith Piaf in 1963, which she had not lived to perform. Out of respect for Piaf, a number of artistes including Dalida had turned it down. Then it had been adapted into English by Mort Schuman, who had written several hits for Elvis Presley and adapted many Jacques Brel classics. Arranged by Schuman, who speeds up the tempo whilst not stinting on the maelstrom of swirling strings it has almost the same introduction as Piaf's "Non, je ne regrette rien", and both technically and vocally remains Cilla's most singularly perfect interpretation. One would almost defy *any* other singer to attempt it, certainly with the same arrangement, and not make a hash of it! A big mistake was George Martin's decision to include Lennon and McCartney's "Yesterday" on the B-side—this is almost as good, and possibly would have given Cilla her third Number One, had it been released separately as an A-side.

The arrangement for "Yesterday" was by Nicky Welsh, Dorothy Squires' orchestra leader, who had signed a short contract to work with Cilla. When George Martin decided that her next single would be Bacharach and David's "Alfie"—the theme from the film of the same name starring Michael Caine—neither she nor Welsh wanted anything to do with the song. Martin put his foot down, and Cilla offered a compromise: she would only record the song if Bacharach flew over from New York to arrange and personally conduct the session! Surprisingly he agreed, and this classy number, released in March (backed with the dreadfully raucous "Night Time Is Here") rocketed to Number 9, and stayed in the charts for over four months. The recording session was filmed, allegedly without Cilla's knowledge. Bacharach the quietly demanding perfectionist goes too far by insisting upon twenty takes—declaring he is still looking for "that little bit of magic". George Martin then tells him that this has already occurred in the fourth take, bringing what has been an exasperating experience to a close. Inexplicably, after all this fuss, Paramount Pictures disapproved of Cilla's recording—pure gold, her voice flows through the complex arrangement like a gently rippling stream, cascading past any obstacles in its path, until reaching its zenith, whence it drops to a whisper—and opted not to include it in the soundtrack of the British print of *Alfie*. For the US release they used the version by Cher. Then to Cilla's horror—she maintained for no other reason than to cause ill-feeling, which may or may not be true, Dionne Warwick recorded the song, selling more copies than anyone else and earning Bacharach and David an Oscar nomination!

On 18 April 1966, Parlophone released *Cilla Sings A Rainbow*, a distinct improvement on its predecessor which reached Number 4 in the charts and sold a million copies in it's first three months. The thirteen songs were all covers, and with one exception—Nicholas Asford and Valerie Simpson's lamentable "The Real Thing", with its squealing repetition of the titular line—equal if not actually better the originals. It opens with her best ever (in this author's opinion!) song, "Love's Just A Broken Heart", and just goes on delivering one thrill after another. Sandy Linzer and Danny Randell's "Lover's Concerto" had been written for The Toys. Based on Bach's *Minuet in G Major*, it had proved a big hit for them—and for one Mrs Miller (1907-97), a latter-day Florence Foster Jenkins who became a sensation *because* she sang so badly! "Make It Easy On Yourself" was more proof that Dionne Warwick was unrivalled when it came to getting gazumped—written for her by Bacharach and David, The Walker Brothers had got there first and taken it to the top of the charts. Cilla sings it with great feeling: had *this* been released as a single, as was suggested at one stage, it would have proved a more than worthy successor to "You've Lost That Loving Feeling". In many respects, George Martin had much to answer for, frequently choosing the wrong single. "One Two Three", written and performed by Len Barry (the Leonard Borisoff in the credits) is belted out here to a superlative orchestration from Nicky Welsh, with Johnny Gray on saxophone.

"Cilla was tremendous to work with," Johnny told me, "A bit tetchy, but like Dot [Squires] such a consummate professional that you forgot the tantrums and just got on with it."

A slight disappointment is Betty Everett's "No Place To Hide"—not on account of Cilla's performance, but because the technician has for some reason opted for a fade-out, which does not happen on the master tape. Side One closes with Victor Young's "When I Fall In Love"—an exercise in sheer perfection which had been gracing Cilla's stage shows of late.

Side Two of this ground-breaking release opens with Arthur Hamilton's "Sing A Rainbow", which had been memorably interpreted by Peggy Lee in *Pete Kelly's Blues*. Peggy, aka the alcoholic gangster's moll who gets beaten up by her thug lover, loses her mind and performs the song after being sectioned to an asylum. Cilla sings it as a lullaby to a child, beautifully and wistfully, her voice at times little more than a whisper. As with the later "Liverpool Lullaby", this one would prove immensely popular with listeners of radio request programmes. Next up is Van McCoy's stunning "Baby I'm Yours", with which Peter and Gordon had a Top Twenty hit in the UK, though after McCoy's tragic early death it was rarely heard by anyone but him. Peter Udell and Gary Geld's "Everything I Touch Turns To Tears" will similarly always be associated with Vikki Carr, though Cilla proves a more than able match for the sob-in-the-voice girl. "In A Woman's Eyes" was currently featuring in Tom Jones' stage show. And finally, there is the obligatory Italian ballad—Mario Panzeri's "My Love Come Home".

There would be many more triumphs during Cilla's lengthy career, but in her recorded work she would rarely match the quality and sheer perfection of *Cilla Sings A Rainbow*.

With Brian Epstein.

With Bobby

Three: I Only Live To Love You

As an all-round entertainer, 1966 would prove Cilla's most successful so far. The successor to "Alfie" should have been Jackie DeShannon's "Only You Can Free My Mind"—DeShannon had written hits for The Searchers, and Marianne Faithfull, and this was a belter of a song. At the last minute, George Martin decided against releasing it and plumped for another Italian standard. "Don't Answer Me" was Nicky Welsh's arrangement of Donatella Moretti's million-selling "Ti vedo uscire". One of the finest ballads Cilla ever sang—the introduction paves the way for the inevitable lump in the throat, and this is *before* she floods her performance with every fibre of her being. Released in March, it reached Number 5 in the charts. During this month, Cilla made a lightning trip to New York where, looking fabulous in a black trouser suit, she received a standing ovation after singing "Love's Just A Broken Heart" on Ed Sullivan's *Toast Of The Town.* She also made her comedy debut in Peter Cook and Dudley Moore's *Not Only But Also*, and on 18 April opened a three-week season of one-woman shows at the Savoy Hotel—not a popular move from the fans' point of view, for they could not afford to see her here. To make up for this, Brian Epstein had the opening night filmed and the hour-long show was broadcast by the BBC in July. The on-stage set up was unusual, in that the orchestra were positioned *behind* her, which meant that *they* had to follow her, and not vice-versa. Few of her contemporaries would have handled such a set up without slipping up, but Cilla with her keen musical ear and astute professionalism got it right every time.

If the critics invariably loved Cilla's singing, *Work Is A Four-Letter Word*—her only feature film, co-starring David

Warner—baffled them. Most major pop stars had attempted the big screen with varying degrees of success: Dave Clark, Cliff Richard, Tommy Steele, The Beatles, Elvis Presley, all with much better efforts than this one. The story—which centres around an eccentric man who creates penis-shaped magic mushrooms—is so far-fetched, it is as if director Peter Hall is making it up as he goes along. The production is unworthy of serious critical analysis, though the film critic from *Variety* would attempt to do so in June 1968:

> There is an irritating air of improvisation about much of the picture which shows up particularly in the editing....The plot and "message" are merely hooks for a series of off-beat situations, some very funny and others over-reminiscent and overstressed. Hall often hangs on to a point just long enough to blunt it. Had he cast the film with expert farce players, it might have turned out very different, almost certainly more amusing and popular....As a thesp [Cilla Black] gets little chance to see her paces, and seems rigidly bewildered by the crazy proceedings around her. Her personality is likeable but unstriking, and the role could have been played by any other young starlet with equal impact.

Other offers of film roles would come winging Cilla's way, but she turned them down—as had happened with Gracie Fields during the Thirties, producers were mostly interested in typecasting her as "the Northern lass", which of course is what she would always be, despite the opulence and riches of the future. All that her incursion into acting achieved, on a personal level, was to make her aware that she was "no Brigitte Bardot or Jean Shrimpton" (her words) and to get her broken nose fixed—though she seems to have been the only one to think there was anything wrong with it. If anything, *en-profile* in *Ferry Cross The Mersey* she looks much more impressive than she would after her operation, which took place in the May on her twenty-fifth birthday. The theme-song for the film, written by Don Black and Guy Wolfenden and sung by Cilla over the credits, later notoriety when Morrissey made arrangements for it to be covered by The Smiths—it appeared on the flipside of their "Girlfriend In A Coma". Morrissey's action, through no fault of Cilla's, part-resulted in the group's split and brought about the outburst from his writing partner, Johnny Marr, "'Work Is A Four-Letter Word' I hated. That was the last straw. I didn't form a group to perform Cilla Black songs!"

Cilla's final single of 1966, released in the October, was "A Fool Am I", Pete Callander's English adaptation of "Dimmelo Parlamo", a big hit in Italy for Fabrizio Ferretti—the singer who had performed "Tu Che Ne Sai" with Dusty at the San Remo Festival. Cilla's take on this is truly exquisite and would have been better if the technician had not opted for a fade-out at the end. On the flipside, and receiving more airplay on some radio stations, was Lennon and McCartney's "For No One". The record reached Number 13 in the charts.

Hopeless as a film star, certainly in the role she had played, Cilla proved a sensation opposite Frankie Howerd in *Way Out In Piccadilly*, a revue written by *Steptoe & Son* creators Ray Galton and Alan Simpson, and comedian Eric Sykes. This opened at the Prince of Wales Theatre on 3 November 1966, and ran until 22 July when Cilla dropped out owing to other work commitments. Her replacement in the revue was Anita Harris. Three weeks later, following an inevitable drop in ticket sales it closed. Indeed, such was the popularity of the Howerd-Black partnership that for a time they became known in the trade as "the celebrities the celebrities want to see", though this was not so in the case of arguably the world's most famous celebrity couple, Elizabeth Taylor and Richard Burton, who saw the show twice—the second time requesting a private meeting with Howerd in his dressing room, where Elizabeth presented him with a pair of matching swords from *Cleopatra*. She made a point of announcing, however, that she had no interest in meeting his co-star.

With Howerd (1917-92) it was a case of opposites attracting: though immensely funny and charismatic on the stage and on television, away from the theatre he was unassuming, very much the introvert and not always easy to get along with, in direct contrast to the unassuming, gregarious singer he befriended. Howerd was sometimes extremely rude towards her, yet she took this in its stride because, she said, he was never malicious. As such he could get away with making fun of her then flat chest by calling her "the girl with two backs", and even refer to her as "an old slapper from Liverpool". Like Brian Epstein, unable to cope with his homosexuality, Howerd was prone to episodes of deep depression. In 1998, Cilla would tell the *Daily Mail*:

> He was the person I went to when not even my husband Bobby could help. When you talked to Frankie, you felt a weight lift off your shoulders. We used to have deep conversations and he'd say, "Don't think I like being gay." He could never bring himself to even mention the word homosexual, but he did say that if he could take a pill to cure him of his 'condition', he would.

The story goes that Cilla and Howerd only met for the first time when he was rehearsing a sketch from the show—and the proceedings were brought to a halt by Cilla's screaming laughter from the back of the darkened auditorium, where he had been secretly watching him. It is highly likely that this *was* just a story, that the two must have met earlier than this to discuss the script. Even so, there was an instant rapport between the two, who would remain close friends for the rest of Howerd's life.

Meanwhile, Brian Epstein was walking his own private path to Calvary, withdrawing more into his shell, rarely socialising with or even checking up on the stars he had launched and nurtured. He attended the opening night of *Way Out In Piccadilly*, but over the next twelve months, Cilla saw little of him. Had she not been so self-obsessed, insisting that everything be centered around her personal universe, she might have realised that his shrinking into the shadows was a call for help. Instead, according to her biographer Douglas Thompson, she accused Epstein of neglecting *her*.

"Cilla complained to Bobby," Thompson observes. "She was as important as The Beatles. She was a star."

Without thinking of the damage which might be inflicted upon Epstein's damaged and fragile psyche, Cilla announced that she was seriously thinking of breaking away from the man who had made her the star she was, so that Bobby could manage her full time.

"It was all to do with money," Nicky Welsh said, "Why should Epstein have his ten-percent when it could stay in the family?"

Cilla and Bobby were invited to discuss the matter at Epstein's Belgravia home, where he pleaded with them not to desert him—even weeping on her shoulder.

"She went from being controlled to being in control," Thompson concludes, "Bobby Willis would always be there, but from then on, Cilla called the shots."

And Nicky Welsh observed, "Brian Epstein helped so many people, some of whom were grateful, many more who were not. When he was down, these people let him stay down. That's what finished him."

Epstein had recently emerged from rehab, where he had undergone treatment for chronic insomnia, amphetamine addiction, and dependency on sleeping pills. Upon seeing how desperate he was Cilla agreed to stay with her manager for the time being—she and Bobby were about to leave for a holiday on the Algarve—but it was too late to save him. She also rejected his offer to put her name forward to represent the UK for the next year's Eurovision Song Contest, claiming that as Sandie Shaw had won this year, the UK would not win again. In the July, Epstein had begun negotiations with the BBC for Cilla to have her own television series—not an easy task, in the days when the North-South divide was stronger than it is today. After some pretty heated arguments, and supported by Cilla's friend, band show legend Billy Cotton, the BBC capitulated and Epstein received news of this on 25 August—by which time Cilla and Bobby were in Portugal. Two days later—on the Saturday of the bank holiday weekend—Epstein was found dead at his London home.

Cilla was heartbroken and, one might suspect, feeling more than a little guilty. The Beatles had been about to re-negotiate their contract with Epstein, and there were rumours that he had been worried that they too might be about to let him go. In Liverpool, in the beginning, Epstein had been surrounded by his self-chosen *famille de coeur*, but escalating world fame and popularity, along with his shrinking further into his shell as the demons took over, had put distance between him and most of them. Other than by telephone, in recent months he had had little contact with any of them. For some time now he had had his finger pressed firmly on the self-destruct button, but such had been his way of hiding his true feelings, until entering rehab no one had realised just how depressed he had become. Epstein had never made a secret of the fact that Cilla and The Beatles had always been his favourites. They had motivated him more than anyone, and the thought of losing them—which he may have interpreted as ingratitude, by even *thinking* about deserting him after all that he had done for them—may have pushed him over the edge.

The coroner's report stated that death had been caused by a lethal cocktail of alcohol, amphetamines and other drugs: even so it was ruled an accidental death—Epstein had been taking so many pills, he had simply lost track of how many he had taken on that fateful day—though the press, and many of those who knew him did not rule out suicide. At the time of his death, not one of his important discoveries was close at hand. Cilla was in Portugal, The Beatles were in Wales with the Maharashi Mahesh Yogi. Gerry & The Pacemakers and the other groups were touring, and only learned of his death from the television news. His mother, Queenie, was at home in Liverpool, having recently lost her husband.

Therefore had Epstein therefore seized the opportunity to end his suffering, knowing that no one would be there to stop him? Or had he in a moment's despair suddenly found the threat of desertion by the artistes he loved too heavy a burden to carry? Or had a male lover threatened him with exposure to the press? If the latter was the case, then what is sad is that, on 28 July 1967, one month before Epstein's death, the House of Commons bill to decriminalise homosexuality for males over the age of twenty-one had received royal assent. Cilla had her own opinion, though critics were swift to point out that she could not discuss her manager's death without involving her ego.

"Brian did not commit suicide," she stressed in *Cilla*, the documentary, "I know it was an accidental death. He was actually found with contracts of mine on the bed. I took great comfort in that....that he was found that way, still more or less caring about me."

Most of Epstein's artistes cancelled at least one concert as a mark of respect. An appearance by wild man rocker Jimi Hendrix at the Saville Theatre, in which Epstein had owned shares, was shelved. Almost everyone also took their time returning to London. During the first twenty-four hours, Scotland Yard detectives did not rule out suspicious play, even though empty pill bottles had been found near the body. Cilla attended his funeral in Liverpool, though Jewish law prevented her from being present at the actual burial. Her last single, some might say the ironically-titled "What Good Am I?" (c/w "Over My Head", both songs my Mort Shuman and Kenny Lynch) had reached Number 24 in the charts a few weeks before Epstein's death. She had been scheduled to record its successor in early September, but the session was put off until the middle of October when she recorded "I Only Live To Love You", Norman Newell's excellent adaptation of Tony Dallava's Italian hit, "Cosi si fa stasera". Dedicated to Bobby, and with an exquisite backing from Sounds Incorporated this one also got no further than Number 26. Both deserved better.

Cilla now had the manager of her choosing, but the appointment had come at a price. In her memoirs, and for no reason, she wonders whether Epstein had found Bobby attractive, and quite unnecessarily states what would have happened, had Epstein ventured to make a move on him:

"He would have got a Liverpool kiss—otherwise known as a 'back-stitch' or head butt—in return."

Cilla also draws attention to "schoolboy boxing champion" Bobby—a man who apparently liked to employ his fists if he felt the need arose—when describing an incident which took place after one of her shows at the Batley Variety Club, during which she had flirted with a man in the audience. This man appears to have taken her seriously, and made advances backstage while she was signing autographs. According to Cilla, who often paints a Neanderthal picture of him, Bobby laid into the man, and:

> When I opened the door there was blood splattered on the walls, on the carpet—everywhere. 'Look at this!' Bobby was saying, 'Look at my new shoes. They're ruined!'

Luckily for Bobby, the man realised the error of his ways and opted not to sue, and the incident did not make the press—though a subsequent punch from Bobby did when, during an altercation in a restaurant, he broke the nose of a drunken "gob-shite" fan who Cilla said had groped her earlier, in the street. Again, the victim did not want to press charges, though the incident did little to enhance Bobby's reputation. Henceforth he would be regarded by some as little more than a thug with an almighty chip on his shoulder.

The last thing Brian Epstein had arranged for Cilla—in the hope that it would prevent her from ditching him—was her first television series, nine shows which ran from January-March 1968. *Cilla* was loosely based on *The Billy Cotton Band Show* (she had often appeared on this) in that it covered all aspects of variety, including comedy sketches with which she would prove particularly adept. Such was her popularity as a television personality that there would be seven more series over the coming years, resulting in her becoming the highest-paid female performer on British television. Being pushy also had its advantages. Wishing to "get one over on her contemporaries"—in other words, Dusty, she had pushed Brian Epstein into securing her fifty minutes of air time for each show, as opposed to the more usual thirty. Also, she insisted upon choosing her own guests, friends and people she liked: Frankie Howerd, Les Dawson, Ringo Starr, Spike Milligan and Henry Mancini. She made a point of telling the press that she and Bobby, and not the BBC, welcomed each guest with a personally signed card and a glass of champagne, *besides* taking them out to dinner afterwards at one of the best eateries in town. Little wonder then, with such boasting that some colleagues began looking down their noses at them.

"Those two were so up themselves that you never quite knew whether to shake their hands, or curtsy," remarked the American jazz singer, Marion Montgomery, "And the way they talked to the 'minions', as Bobby referred to the technicians, was sometimes nothing short of shameful."

To show that there were no hard feelings or any rivalry between them, Cilla insisted upon inviting Sandie Shaw, Marianne Faithfull, Lulu and Dusty Springfield to appear on her show. In her memoirs she enthuses over Sandie's long legs and bare feet, Marianne's "captivating natural beauty", and Lulu's "amazing lungs". She is however somewhat sanctimonious when discussing Dusty. Having drawn attention to her "gorgeous blonde hair and panda eyes" she makes a point of writing that Dusty lives with another woman—"I know, shocking,"—and comments how Dusty once invited her and Bobby to a party, "To convince her parents that she had some sane, normal, non-gay friends!" She even has the gall to add, "I think she learned a few things from me—not vocally so much, more in terms of dress sense."

This was nonsense and, as Kris Kirk explained to me, wishful thinking on Cilla's part:

> Cilla liked to think that Dusty loved her to bits. The truth is, Dusty confided in me that she couldn't stand the mortal sight of her or that boorish, homophobic husband of hers. I think everybody knew, too, that Cilla was more than a little peeved because Dusty made in the States, when she did not.

Another star who Cilla rubbed up the wrong was Gracie Fields. Prior to her first television show, she received a telegram from Gracie, in Capri.

"Gracie considered her one of the worst singers she had ever heard," her Rochdale friend Mary Whipp said. "But Cilla was due to fly out to Capri to discuss a possible film portrayal of Gracie's early life, so Gracie sent the telegram just to be polite."

The proposed film was a doomed project from the start, because the producer wanted to use Cilla's singing voice as opposed to miming to Gracie's, which Gracie's fans would never have tolerated no matter how good she might have been, and for which she would almost certainly been severely criticised by the media. Gracie, who never retired, had lived at her Canzone del Mare complex on Capri for over thirty years. It was *TV Times* who financed Cilla and Bobby's trip out to the island for a photoshoot-interview, even though she was about to appear on the cover of its rival, *Radio Times*.

Gracie had heard of Cilla's boasts that comparisons had been made between them, and Douglas Thompson recalls her having told one photographer:

> She wants to be me, even before I'm in my grave. She's awful. What a dreadful person she is. She obviously doesn't care about anybody but herself. Look at the way she treats people!

Over the phone, Gracie told her stepdaughter, Irene Bevan:

> She and her husband remind me of the Formbys. And she was definitely Beryl, with all her phoney airs and graces. While she was here on Capri she treated some people like something you've scraped off your shoe, and as soon as she opened her mouth it was like sitting next to a fog-horn. I told Boris [Gracie's third husband], 'There's no way I'm having that woman playing me and squawking *my* songs down her nose and having everybody think I'm as horrible in real life as she is!

With Cilla out of the picture, Gracie suggested that maybe she should be portrayed by Maggie Smith, Susan Maughan, or Patricia Routledge. The latter entered into talks with the BBC, but the film was never made.

Cilla's ultimate insult to Gracie came a few years later. In her memoirs, she observes:

> I saw Gracie Fields, in Capri before she died. I went to see her at 11 am with the sun blazing down—and she was singing the words of her song, *Sally, Sallyyyyy*. I turned to Bobby and begged him, "Don't ever let me get like that."

There would be no danger of this ever happening. Cilla Black was a great entertainer, of this there is no doubt, but she never had been and never would be in the same league as the woman revered as "Our Gracie".

During this winter of 1967-8, Cilla spent a great deal of time in one studio or another—taping her television series, which regularly drew in at least 12 million viewers, and working on her new album, *Sher-oo!*, released in the April.

With this, she almost makes a return to the mish-mash of her debut album—though this one reached Number 7 in the charts, it seemed that there was little accounting for taste, for there were more mediocre songs than good ones. The cover was also un-Cilla-like—gone, temporarily, is the bobbed look in favour of a fluffy perm which makes her look remarkably like the "It" girl, silent movies star Clara Bow. It opens with Bacharach and David's "What The World Needs Now Is Love", which they had written for Jackie DeShannon, and for once the cover version by Dionne Warwick is better than both. The number begins with what could be mistaken as a child playing a trumpet very badly—short, tuneless, willy-nilly blasts—and does not improve when Cilla ups the tempo. As usual, there has to be at least one Italian song for this to be an authentic Cilla Black album, and she excels herself as always with "Suddenly You Love Me"—a hit for Ricardo Del Turco as "Uno tranquilo". "This Is The First Time" was from the hit-writing team of Doug Flett and Guy Fletchers: one of their compositions, "Wonderful World", was sung by Cliff Richard in the "Song For Europe" segment of Cilla's television show, and was later recorded by Elvis Presley. After the so-so "Follow The Path Of The Stars" comes Tim Hardin's "Misty Roses", from his classic *Reason To Believe* album. Cilla performs it with great tenderness, a far cry from her horrendous calypso-beat squalling in Gladys Knight & The Pips "Take Me In Your Arms And Love Me"—the backing singers on this, fighting to out-shriek Cilla, instinctly have one reaching for the skip button.

"Yo-Yo", The Osmonds' hit which opens Side Two, is poor. Quite exceptional on the other hand—one wonders who was responsible for choosing the songs for this album when they vary so much in quality—is Roger Greenaway and Roger Cook's "Something's Gotten Hold Of My Heart".

Originally recorded by the pair in their guise of David and Jonathan, it had also proved a massive hit for Gene Pitney. Cilla's may have the better (Johnny Harris) orchestration, but in trying to keep up with this she over-reaches on the top notes and the result—particularly towards the end—is a near-disaster. Next up is Paul McCartney's "Step Inside Love", which also sees John Lennon's name in the credits, though he is not thought to have had any input at all. Cilla performed the song—which McCartney later said had been composed in the bathroom—as an opener for her television series, and never intended recording it until fans began calling the BBC to ask where they could find it. Cilla recorded it and it was released on 9 March, peaking at Number 8 in the charts—by which time the series had ended! It proved unintentionally controversial when an Australian DJ refused to play it, protesting that the lyrics referred to prostitution and venereal disease, in particular the lines, "Let me find you a place, Where the curse [sic] of the day will be carried away by the smile on your face." In fact, the problem lay with Cilla's Liverpool accent—the way she had pronounced the word "cares"! Then, after a tedious rendition of Francis Lai's "A Man And A Woman" comes Bobby's and Clive Westlake's "I Couldn't Take My Eyes Off You"—followed by a truly inspirational reading of Paddy Roberts' 1959 scouting ditty, "Follow Me". Roberts (1910-75) was something of a cross between French *chansonnier* Georges Brassens and Benny Hill, and known for risqué lyrics, such as "The Ballad Of Bethnal Green", which frequently cropped up on *The Benny Hill Show*. Cilla's interpretation is pure magic. "When you were a little wolf cub and I was a brownie," she sings, before recounting her Jamboree adventure which ends, "You wanted to be a boy scout so you could salute me—with three fingers vertical instead of just two!"

1968 was not a prolific year for record releases, owing to Cilla's other work commitments. In the June, Parlophone released "Where Is Tomorrow"—as "Non 'ce Domani", this had been written and introduced by Umberto Bindi, the man responsible for "You're My World". The flipside, to coincide with the release of the film, was Guy Woolfenden and Don Black's "Work Is A Four-Letter Word". There is no way of explaining why, despite the sheer genius of Cilla's interpretation, the record got no further than Number 39 in the charts. It deserved much better than this.

The Bindi song aside, Cilla's best songs at this time were the "leftovers" from the *Sher-oo!* sessions, four of which were released on an EP, *Time For Cilla*—an unusual move in that in those days EPs usually contained hits from previous singles. "Abyssinian Secret" and the wistful "Trees And Loneliness" were penned by teenagers Simone Avadis and Earl Okin, who had worked with Helen Shapiro—singer-songwriter Okin recorded for The Beatles' Apple label. "Time", performed as a neo-*fado*, was written by Norman Newell and George Martin. The pièce de resistance, however, was Robert Livraghi's "There I Go". Originally titled "Se per te c'e soltanto quell'uomo", it had been recorded by Shirley Bassey and Vikki Carr—the reason why Martin balked at releasing it as a single. The song's range is quite extraordinary, not to mention the key changes. Cilla handles it all effortlessly—in what is probably her best Italian song after "You're My World".

One ravishing song which slipped through the net was "Your Heart Is Free Like The Wind". Composed by Christian Chevalier and performed by a French ensemble, Les Troubadours, "Le vent et la jeunesse" was awarded the prestigious *Rose d'Or d'Antibes* in 1967. The English adaptation has lyrically little in common with the original. Cilla is thought to have sung, and may even have recorded, the French version. Why George Martin decided against putting out this gem as a single—or even on an album—is quite frankly baffling.

On 25 January 1969, Cilla and Bobby—it was his twenty-seventh birthday—were married at the Marylbone Registry Office, surprising their friends who had expected them to just go on living together. She quotes his typical proposal—"Well, what d'you reckon? Do you want to do it or not?"—and the rush to organise the ceremony. She wore a red velvet high-wasted dress which she had bought off the peg for ten guineas from a King's Road boutique, carried a simple bunch of anemone, and looked stunning. Her wish not to have her parents at her wedding was granted—it had been her intention, she said, to tell them about it afterwards, no doubt when it was too late for them to talk her out of it. As devout Catholics the Whites would not have recognised any marriage not taking place in a church. What Cilla had not reckoned on was the media—Cilla Sr. heard the news on the radio and was understandably upset. What was said about the bride wearing red is not on record. The event was low-key: just a handful of close friends. Bobby's best man, despite his obvious homophobia, was Saville Row tailor Tommy Nutter: his partner, Brian Epstein's former assistant Peter Brown, gave the bride away. Cathie McGowan was matron of honour. The reception—Cilla's idea of keeping things simple—took place at the Ritz. There was no honeymoon: she was too busy taping her television series and working on a new album.

Under pressure from her family, Cilla agreed to a second wedding in a church. Her mother had wanted this to take place at Liverpool Cathedral, nicknamed Paddy's Wigwam. The authorities refused: by living in sin and by marrying at a registry office, she was told, she had set a bad example for decent Catholic girls. A compromise was reached when a priest at the Whites' local church, in Woolton, agreed to a lunchtime blessing on 6 March. Given away by her father, Cilla wore a white dress trimmed with ostrich feathers. This time, the bridesmaids were dressed in scarlet.

Surely it must have been by way of sheer coincidence that, between Cilla's two weddings, Parlophone released "Surround Yourself With Sorrow" as her new single! Also, just as there was no logical explanation why her last single had flopped, one might ask why this one—very poor in comparison—sailed to Number 3 in the charts. Written by Bill Martin and Phil Coulter (whose "Puppet On A String" had won Eurovision) and catchy as it may be, it contains arguably one of the silliest lines in any Sixties song "What do you do when your love breaks up—fall apart like a buttercup?" Far better is the flipside—Bobby's and Clive Westlake's "London Bridge", a nice, visual piece wherein the narrator laments her recently removed favourite landmark, the place where she met the love of her life.

Surround Yourself With Cilla was released at the end of May, and saw a return to form after the hodgepodge of *Sher-oo!* The sessions were conducted by former Manfred Mann member Mike Vickers, and produced works of such impeccable quality that one rues the fact that he and Cilla did not collaborate more often. The album opens with a rip-roaring "Aquarius" from the musical. *Hair*, which leads nicely into Harry Nilsson's "Without Him" (recorded by Jack Jones as "Without Her" and not to be confused with the frequently raucous "Without You", by the same singer-composer). "Only Forever Will Do" was an Italian pop song (as opposed to one of Cilla's essential ballads), but an inordinately good one, faithful to the original ("Prigionerio del mondo) by Lucio Battisti (1943-98), one of the most influential Continental singer-songwriters of his day. Battisti, a feisty individual, refused to allow George Martin permission to use Cilla's version of his song until he had listened to the master tape. When he heard this, he was so impressed with her voice that he suggested she should record an English adaptation of his million-selling "Mi retorni in mente". Sadly, this never happened. Cilla's impressive reading of Bacharach and David's "You'll Never Get To Heaven If You Break My Heart" sees her not just covering the Dionne Warwick song, but also apparently trying to imitate her voice—and still coming off best! The album's other highlights are her take on The Bee Gees' "Words", far better than the "nanny-goat" original—and an astonishingly infectious version of "Red Rubber Ball", unquestionably Cilla's best commercially released song this year. Written by Paul Simon, with Bruce Woodley of The Seekers, who covered it, this had taken The Cyrkle to Number 2 in the US charts.

Hot on the heels of the new album was Cilla's next single: Greenaway's and Cook's "Conversations", at just over four minutes an unusually long song when most radio stations limited each record to three minutes of airplay. Motown-esque, its musical mood changes with each stanza, and as usual Cilla triumphs with a difficult arrangement. Her penultimate Top Ten hit, it peaked at Number 7 in the charts. There was also an interesting Italian language version of the song, backed with "Without Him". By coupling the song with Stan Kelly-Bootle's "Liverpool Lullaby", however, George Martin was doing himself and Cilla a dis-service: this tragi-comic masterpiece, written and performed in the Liverpool dialect, certainly deserved to be an A-side. It tells the story of a poverty-stricken young mother who scrimps and saves, while her husband boozes away what little money is coming into the house. All will turn out well, though—so long as they win the football pools, whence the drunken husband will be able to have a brewery of his own—and she concludes, "Go to sleep for your Mammy" Some believed at the time that Cilla, with her fondness for the champagne lifestyle, was the wrong interpreter of such a number. And yet one cannot possibly anyone else singing it, let alone with such utter conviction. "Oh, you are a mucky kid," Cilla soothes her rapscallion child, before admonishing him with, "When he sees the things you did, you'll gerra belt from your dad!" For many years, it would be played on radio request programmes long after "Conversations" had been forgotten. Today it is banned from many radio stations who claim that it "advocates parental violence". Whenever Cilla performed the song in her later years, "gerra belt" was changed to "get told off", and the football pools had given way to the lottery. How times have changed, and some might argue not for the better!

In 10 November, Cilla appeared in her second *Royal Variety Performance*. Gracie Fields had topped the bill last time: now it was Danny La Rue and Ginger Rogers. The star who made the biggest impression however was French singing sensation Mireille Mathieu. Cilla's final single of the decade, released that month, was John Cameron's "If I Thought You'd Ever Change Your Mind"—a semi-surreal piece which peaked at a modest Number 20 in the charts. On the flipside was a nifty little German drinking song: Werner Scharfenberger's "It Feels So Good".

Cilla *was* feeling good. Indeed, if not necessarily so far as chart successes were concerned, things could not have been better. She had just found out that she was pregnant.

Four: Tantrums & Tears

With the dawning of the new decade, Cilla like the other Brit Girls saw a lull in her chart career. Her next album, *Sweet Inspiration*, recorded during the winter of 1969-70, only reached Number 42 in the charts. It has its moments—some quite good ones, in fact. Cilla gives a very gentle but effective reading of Joni Michell's "Both Sides Now", and a passable one of Ron Miller's "For Once In My Life", a hit in the UK for Dorothy Squires. "Put A Little Love In Your Heart was from the pen of Jackie DeShannon. "Black Paper Roses" is the allegorical story of the unloved child who forgives its mother for deserting it, though we are not sure if the child is still alive or speaking from beyond the grave. The song was written by Belle Gonzalez who despite the name was a British jazz singer-musician and contemporary of Nick Drake. In view of what happened a few years later, however, one cannot imagine Cilla wishing to reflect on an albeit beautiful plaintiff which begins, "And I hark sorrow to my mind, as a mother to her breast a stillborn child." Bizarre is John Lennon's "Across The Universe", written in the wake of his Transcendental meditation experiences with the Maharashi Mahesh Yogi. Only he knew exactly what the lyrics were about. This said, Cilla handles the material well, taking great care over the pronunciation of the much-repeated holy Sanskrit phrase, "*Jai guru deva om,*"—"Hail to the divine guru," the elongated "*ommm*" referring to the cosmic sound of the universe, as chanted by monks. Profound stuff!

Cilla's only single of 1970, "Child Of Mine", did not chart. Yet though there would be just one more excursion into the Top Twenty, she was able to celebrate the fact that while The Beatles had split up and other Merseyside groups were quickly fading from view, she was "still up there on stage and on TV." Her pregnancy had not been planned, and one press report estimated that her confinement would cost her over £10,000 in lost fees from cancelled television work and the postponing of an overseas tour. Yet from her point of view this was but a small price to pay for the privilege of starting a family. Her first son, Robert—named after his father—was born in the exclusive Avenue Clinic, St John's Wood, on 26 July 1970.

A few weeks later, Cilla, Bobby and the new arrival moved into a 17-room Edwardian mansion in Denham, Buckinghamshire. Set in 17 acres of landscaped gardens and woodland, it was a large house for their rapidly increasing family. There may only have been one baby so far, but between them the couple would soon have amassed twelve dogs, two horses, and dozens of budgerigars and cockatiels! They paid just over £40,000 for the property in which Cilla lived until her death. And yet, she and Bobby were never accepted by the locals, who over the years accused them of being standoffish. Whenever anyone from Denham was asked about Cilla Black, their comments were invariably negative—offensive, at times. So too were their actions. When Bobby decided to add a lake to the property, assuming that this would be classed as additional landscaping to the grounds, he just went ahead. One of the neighbours, rather than have the courtesy to inform him that he would need planning permission from the local council to do this, waited until the work was completed before reporting him. Subsequently, Bobby had forked out a huge amount of money for nothing.

This antagonism stemmed from Cilla keeping herself to herself, and of course in such situations where busybodies are concerned, lack of information often inevitably leads to speculation. She had moved into the house to afford herself and her family as much privacy as possible—Bobby once said, "So as not to have some old biddy knocking on the door to ask us to open the church fete."

Cilla was more direct, when asked about her neighbours, and some of the things they had said about her: "I don't hit back—and in any case, I wouldn't know any of them if I fell over them."

Several times she urged her parents to move to Denham so that she could be close to them, but they always refused. Their sons and the rest of their family all lived in Liverpool.

The record sales had dropped off, but as a television, concert and pantomime star Cilla was more popular than ever. Even without spending time in the charts, the *New Musical Express* voted her Top British Female Vocalist. She had matured into a fine family entertainer and had begun ascending the ladder which would see her crowned queen in an entertainments sphere which did not measure success in revolutions-per-minute.

1971 saw sell-out concerts up and down the country, a record-breaking season at Blackpool Opera House—and at the end of the year, her last major hit. "Something Tells Me" had replaced "Step Inside Love" as the theme for her television series, and peaked at Number 3 in the charts. In time it would be replaced by the less endearing "Baby, We Can't Go Wrong". The series ran until 1976 (with maternity breaks in 1970, 1972 and 1975) and regularly attracted 13 million viewers. There was also heartbreak when, halfway through the Blackpool season, Cilla suffered a miscarriage. Then, in 1972, her father died after a lengthy illness.

"My faith was rocked for the first time," she said, "I said over and over to God, *'Go away—I've fallen out with you.'*"

Cilla and Bobby's second son, Ben, was born on 30 April 1974 at Queen Charlotte's Hospital, in Hammersmith.

Her television career took a successful swing in another direction when she appeared in a sit-com, *Cilla's Comedy Six*, for ITV. Aired in January 1975, this comprised six thirty-minute episodes, with her playing a different part in each: many of her co-stars were from the cast of *Coronation Street*. Like her variety series, this fared well in the ratings despite being panned by the critics, and a second series was commissioned: *Cilla's World Of Comedy* would be aired during the autumn of 1976. The UK Writer's Guild named her Top British Female Comedy of the Year.

Heartbreak, however, was once again just around the corner when, on 4 October 1975, Cilla gave birth to her third baby—a two months premature daughter, Ellen, who lived just a few hours. One cannot even begin to imagine how devastated she and Bobby must have felt.

"I felt as if my life had drained away with her," she recalled, "I was inconsolable, riddled with guilt, enmeshed in a depression from which I was convinced there was no return."

Cilla was midway through a season in Coventry when the tragedy occurred and once she had recovered from the worst of the ordeal, she returned to work. The love and applause of her fans helped, though she found it impossible to perform "Liverpool Lullaby", which was temporarily removed from her repertoire. To help others who had suffered the anguish of losing a child, she began raising funds for Birthright. Her first television appeal brought in enough money to buy a heart monitor for the hospital where Ellen had died.

At the end of 1978, Cilla was halfway through a *Dick Whittington* season at the Liverpool Empire when she and Bobby were involved in a car accident. A vehicle travelling in the wrong direction skidded on black ice and swerved towards them, and only Bobby's quick thinking saved them from serious injury. Later on in the run the show was halted by an IRA bomb scare. Pretending to be calm, Cilla asked the audience to look under seats for suspect packages, whilst security men searched the rest of the theatre. When nothing was found, she announced, "If you want to stay, you're welcome—because *we're* staying!" One journalist likened her stance with that of the Queen Mother, when she had refused to leave London during the Blitz.

Cilla reduced her workload upon learning that she was pregnant again, refusing to travel anywhere by plane unless absolutely necessary. Her third son, Jack, was born on 20 October 1980. Soon afterwards, she and Bobby travelled to the Arab Emirates and it was here, on 8 December—her mother's birthday—that she heard the news that John Lennon had been shot dead by a fanatic in New York. That evening, she finished the show with his "Imagine".

"It was as if a bright, shining light had been turned off," she said.

In 1982, Stephen Barnard wrote in *The History of Rock*:

> The key to Cilla Black's continuing popularity with the family audience is her homely image and her apparent loyalty to her Northern roots....Musically, Cilla was never an important figure, but what she *did* have was a gauche charm that belied a serious professionalism. As the only Epstein protegé to establish a lasting career for herself, she ultimately survived by keeping the essence of her image and appeal intact.

In the wake of an appearance on *Wogan* in January 1983, which saw her taking over the proceedings and having the audience in stitches, Cilla's television career took off like a rocket when London Weekend Television contracted her to host *Surprise, Surprise!* The theme of the programme involved surprising members of the public by making long dreamed-of wishes come true, and reuniting them with long-lost loved ones. The first show, which went out on 6 May 1984, saw Cilla triumphing over extreme adversity. She had been experiencing dizzy spells for a while, and now began haemorrhaging internally—just days before the live broadcast she underwent a blood transfusion. Doctors had discovered a growth, and a few weeks later she underwent a hysterectomy.

With typical sardonic Northern humour, she recalled how she had told Bobby, "They've taken away the nursery, and left the playpen."

The indomitable trooper, Cilla was back on her feet in no time: between now and December 2001 there would be 137 60-minute episodes of *Surprise, Surprise!* attracting a minimum 12 million viewers every Sunday evening. Even more popular was *Blind Date*, which frequently overlapped with *Surprise, Surprise!* and ran from November 1985 until April 2003—18 series, a total of 356 episodes. Based on an Australian game show it featured a trio of same-sex singletons who, heard but not seen by a member of the opposite sex, were asked a series of sometimes risqué questions with a view to choosing which one to take on a blind date. They were given a choice of three envelopes, to decide where to go for this—what viewers did not know was that all three envelopes contained the same destination —and the following week, they reported back on their adventure, which had been filmed. Most of the participants ended up never wanting to see each other again, but there were happy endings and at least one wedding, attended by Cilla. The programme introduced several catchphrases, such as "lorra lorra laughs", and each contestant was addressed by her as "our" whoever. The series ended when

Cilla announced during a live episode that she was leaving: though several A-list presenters were considered to take over, the programme was cancelled quite simply because she was irreplaceable.

The retrospectives and compilations aside, the albums between 1971 and 1990 displayed Cilla's (and her record companies) knack of distinguishing between good and bad when it comes to a choice of material. This is either inordinately good, or downright dire—rarely between. This difference in quality may be best illustrated by listening to the 2003 collection, *Cilla: The Best of 1963-78*. The 80 songs are presented in no particular order, therefore we have horrors like "Take Me In Your Arms And Love Me" sandwiched between "What Good Am I?" and "Love Of The Loved" and worse still, "Without You" following "Red Rubber Ball". Shockingly, there is just one song by Bobby Willis, who could have taught some of the better-known composers a thing or two about songwriting.

In *Images* (1971) there is the most fantastic version of Elton John's "Your Song", whereas Cilla makes a complete hash of Simon & Garfunkel's "Bridge Over Troubled Water". *Day By Day With Cilla* (1973), her final album for Parlophone, sees her getting her revenge on Cher for gazumping her with "Alfie" by offering a far superior version of her "Gypsies, Tramps And Thieves", whilst Harry Nilsson's "Without You" attains new heights of mediocrity—Cilla's top notes in this one are not just overtly strained, they are excruciatingly painful to endure. Almost as bad is her tiny voice approach to Lennon & McCartney's "The Long And Winding Road". Her take on "I Don't Know How To Love Him" in *It Makes Me Feel Good,* leaves little to be desired, yet Alex Harvey's "I'll Take A Tango"—like the earlier "Follow Me" supposed to be funny—is without any doubt the *worst* thing she ever sang.

One can almost visualise the subject of the song, Rudolph Valentino, turning in his grave. *In My Life* (1974), Cilla's debut album for EMI, contains just one decent song—Terry Dempsey's "Daydreamer", which though covered by David Cassidy, arguably belongs to French heartthrob Claude Francois, who sold more copies (as "Le mal aimé) than all the others added together.

In the midst of this hit-and-miss jumble, Cilla recorded "Little Things Mean A Lot", a chart-topper on both sides of the Atlantic for Kitty Kallen—and Jackie DeShannon's "When You Walk Into The Room", a Top Five hit back in 1965 for The Searchers. Two undisputed gems, the former was released as a single and did not chart, whilst the DeShannon song ended up in the EMI archives until 2003. Then, it was back to the duffers. *Modern Priscilla* (1978), produced by former Springfield Tom Hurst, and *Especially For You*, plunge the very depths of mediocrity—the latter album, released on the K-Tel label proved that there was no accounting for taste by achieving silver disc status, and is a collection of lukewarm middle-of-the-road standards with which she makes no effort whatsoever to sound like the Cilla of old. There is no depth of feeling, no attempt to even reach for that enigmatic upper register. This is the sort of record one would expect to hear, and ignore, in airport lounges and doctors' waiting rooms where any sound is better than the tedium of having to be there.

1985's *Surprisingly Cilla*, on the other hand, offers a complete volt-face: an amazing collection *because* it represents Cilla, proving herself still a force to be reckoned with, taking a welcome trip down memory lane. Included here are "Surprise, Surprise!", "I Know Him So Well", and fabulous re-recordings of "You're My World" and "Step Inside Love". Then it is a return to dross with *Cilla's World* (1990) an Australian release of instantly forgettable, mostly animal-themed piffle which is probably best ignored.

The concert appearances, though by now less frequent, were another matter. Rather than the new material the fans always wanted the big hits and Italian ballads with which she could do no wrong. she gave a memorable performance —one which in common with the other participants she wished might not be taking place—at the Liverpool Empire to benefit the families of the Hillsborough Disaster. On 15 April 1989, mere minutes into the FA Cup semi-final clash between Liverpool and Nottingham Forest, 94 fans were crushed to death at the Hillsborough Stadium, in Sheffield. Another fan died soon afterwards and Tony Bland attracted headline news around the world by living on in a permanent vegetative state until 1993, when he became the first British person suffering from the condition to have his life-support switched off. Cilla sang "Alfie", reduced the audience to tears with "Liverpool Lullaby", and joined the other performers in the "You'll Never Walk Alone" finale. The song from *Carousel*, reprised by Gerry & The Pacemakers, had been adopted by Liverpool as their anthem.

That same year, Cilla's youngest son, 9-year-old Jack, was seriously injured when he cycled into a tree near his home. She was appearing in *Aladdin* at the Wimbledon Theatre, and found herself criticised for continuing with the show that evening rather than rushing to his bedside with Bobby. Fortunately, Jack pulled through.

The following September, Cilla attracted more bad press on account of her eldest son, Robert, whose car collided with a motorcycle in Denham, ridden by 25-year-old social-worker Richard Potter, who subsequently died of his injuries, resulting in Robert facing a dangerous driving charge. Cilla was torn between two poles: helping her son through his ordeal whilst offering support to the dead man's family without her celebrity status getting in the way. Unfairly, she received hate mail, whilst the press accused her of monopolising on the tragedy by referring to the accident during a charity luncheon, and breaking down in tears. So as not to turn the event into a media circus, she refused to accompany Robert to the hearing, where Richard Potter's death was ruled an accident. Robert was fined, and his license endorsed for "not being a reasonable and prudent driver".

Whilst this drama was being played out in an aggressive media spotlight, on 18 April 1992 Cilla suffered her third upset in less than three years when Frankie Howerd died of a heart-attack, aged 75. It was she and his long-term partner, Dennis Haymer, who led the tributes at his memorial service at London's St-Martin-in-the-Fields, two weeks later.

"I'm just very proud to have known him," she told the congregation, fighting back the tears, "I could talk for a trillion years about Frankie, and never get bored."

In 1993 came the triple revelation that was *Through The Years*, a celebration of Cilla's thirty years in the business, which coincided with her fiftieth birthday. There was a picture book, and a video: interviewed at home by Paul Gambaccini, Cilla spoke candidly of her life and career, and there were full-length clips of her singing her hits, on stage at the Savoy Hotel. The album, a mini-masterpiece, was produced by Charlie Skarbek and Rick Blaskey, who wrote two of the songs. Featured on it and the television special which followed were "friends" who had agreed to duet with her, though allegedly only Cliff Richard was regarded as such. The album opens with Skarbek and Blaskey's title-track, in which Cilla takes a trip down memory lane: she recalls love songs on the radio, and refers to her favourite Beatles songs, films she loved, dreams that she had back then. Her first *Top of the Pops* in fifteen years pushed the song into the lower reaches of the charts. Then comes the duet with Cliff—Burt Bacharach's "That's What Friends Are For", followed by The Beatles' "Here, There And Everywhere". The most talked about song on the album was her duet with Dusty Springfield—Skarbek and Blaskey's "Heart And Soul"—the fact that these so-called rivals had finally buried the hatchet and opted to perform together. In fact, it was Starbek who persuaded Dusty to appear on the album, enabling the session to take place in an atmosphere of alleged bonhomie. Similarly Cilla's duet with Barry Manilow—"You'll Never Walk Alone", which sees her almost drowning him—came about not because either party had ever expressed a need to work with the other, but because one of the surprises on Cilla's television show had involved an impromptu visit to a Manilow concert, where the two had ended up on stage together. Indeed, though through no fault of Cilla's, this is the only poor performance on the album. Regardless of its origins, to her way of thinking this was a Liverpool song, and would have benefitted the input of one of her Merseyside colleagues—Gerry Marsden, for instance—rather than the flat, dull tones of Manilow. That same year, at the Royal Variety Performance, Cilla brought the house down when she led the entire cast into the song for the show's finale.

For *Through The Years*, Cilla re-recorded "Anyone Who Had A Heart" and "You're My World", proving beyond the shadow of a doubt that she could still "knock 'em cold" with a heartfelt ballad. Also her upper register—whilst having lost none of its power—is perfectly controlled and less nasal than back in 1964. She also included the most amazing versions of Ralph McTell's "Streets Of London" (accompanied by him on guitar), and Julie Gold's "From A Distance". Words defy the brilliance of Peter van Asten and

Richard Debois' "A Dream Come True". As "Ik hou van jou" and performed by Maribelle, this had been the Dutch entry for the 1964 Eurovision Song Contest. The song had come a paltry 13th but had gone on to become a classic—in France, it had been recorded by Serge Lama. Cilla's version sees her accompanied on the grand piano by Charlie Starbek. The album however was not the success everyone anticipated it would be, stalling at Number 41 in the charts, though it has since caught up, sales-wise, with her classic albums from the Sixties.

Cilla hit the headlines again, for all the wrong reasons, at the end of 1997 when Channel Four were scheduled to broadcast their *Brit Girls* series. The producers had commissioned five 60-minute programmes—one each about Cilla, Marianne, Lulu, Sandie Shaw, and a final retrospective covering one-hit wonders. Why Dusty was not included was not explained. According to Cilla, whose interviews were filmed at some length for use in all five programmes, the producers had told her that there would be one documentary only—about her. For the detractors, and even for some fans, this was arrogance and one-upmanship at its highest level when Cilla's lawyers sued the television company for £70,000, claiming that she had been conned into making a programme which included other British female singers—her way of saying, or so they interpreted, that these other women were of less importance than her. The matter was referred to the High Court, as a result of which the title of the documentary featuring her was changed to *Cilla*—the other programmes had their dates moved forwards, according to a Channel Four spokesman, "To put some distance between the Queen and the underlings." The tabloids were ruthless, and one attacked her by way of one of her own catchphrases—"Mrs. Lorra Lorra Ego".

From now on, the tabloids would be looking for the slightest excuse to "bring her down a peg or two". That same year when her Aunt Mary was discovered to be living in "near-destitute" conditions in Liverpool it was Cilla—the "millionairess who lived like royalty"—who copped the blame. No one mentioned the fact that she had worked hard for her fortune, and thoroughly merited it. "I expect Cilla could afford to buy me a nice little cottage in the country," Aunt Mary told the *News of the World*, bringing an attack from Liverpool City Council, who accused Cilla of making a living from the city of her birth, whilst never bothering to visit—untrue, of course. Then, proving herself nothing less than a trouble-causing, contrary old woman, Mary White told the *Sunday Mirror*, "Even if she offered to buy me a cottage, I would tell her that I'm happy where I am!" It had all been a completely unnecessary smear campaign: Cilla had last seen Aunt Mary in 1996 (at her mother's funeral), and even then for the first time in some thirty years!

The bottom dropped out of Cilla's world during the summer of 1999, when Bobby was diagnosed with cancer. She too had had a scare, a few years earlier, when she had developed a lump in her breast: this had been speedily dealt with, the lump had been removed, and she had been given the all clear. Cilla was smack in the middle of a new game show series, *Moment Of Truth*—airing between September 1998 and September 2001, this involved her visiting three families each week at their homes and setting them tasks, mental or physical, then returning the following week to see how they had fared, and to award them fantastic prizes. She had completed the first series, and in the May had collected her OBE from Buckingham Palace—"for services rendered to stage and television". In some photographs, Bobby had looked gaunt. The couple were holidaying in the West Indies when he complained of feeling unusually tired.

Tests carried out at Oxford's Nuffield Hospital revealed an inoperable tumour on his liver. He deteriorated rapidly: his kidneys started to fail, and he developed pneumonia. And during the afternoon of 23 October, Bobby passed away in his sleep at London's Free Hospital. He was only 57.

Within a week of Bobby's funeral, Cilla was back on the *Blind Date* set—the trooper inside demanding that, yet again, the show must go on. Some of the tabloids showed her no mercy, claiming that her marriage had been a sham—little more than a business arrangement. What rot! In forty years, they had spent just four nights apart—when Cilla had had her children—and were lasting proof that some show business marriages *did* work. Now, she said, she would dedicate the rest of her life to serving Bobby's memory. She even declared, after taking her first plane without him by her side, that she was no longer afraid of flying because if the plane crashed, she wanted to join him.

On 28 November 2001, Cilla appeared in the Royal Variety Performance, her first time on stage in eight years. She teamed up with drag queen Lily Savage (aka her friend Paul O'Grady) and *Carry On* star Barbara Windsor, and they stole the show and even had the Queen clutching her side with laughter. With their 10-minutes sketch from *Gypsy*, wearing basques and singing "You Gotta Have A Gimmick", the trio portrayed ageing strippers who teach an unseen pupil how it should be done. Cilla raised the roof with her flashing-lights bra, bottom, and crotch—faking an orgasm and bringing the impromptu comment from Savage, "Mind you don't singe yourself!"—with Cilla surprising even herself that she had pulled off such a stunt, and with such good taste.

At almost sixty, Cilla had lost none of her innate magic The voice was still there, setting her in good stead for a belated career on the musical comedy stage, providing this was what she wanted. The following spring, she took a step in this direction when she appeared at London's Wyndham Theatre in *The Play What I Wrote*, a celebration of the work of Morecambe and Wise, directed by Kenneth Branagh. Each evening, a surprise guest did a turn", and Cilla walked on stage wearing a long satin dressing gown which she shed to reveal a still shapely pair of pins in a black, spangled leotard before joining the ensemble in Eric and Ernie's signature tune, "Bring Me Sunshine". The audiences loved her yet it would take several more years to tread the boards again. Her final performances took place at the end of 2008, when Liverpool was designated the Capital of European Culture. Rounding off the year's events was the city's costliest pantomime ever—*Cinderella*, a £1 million extravaganza with local celebrity Jennifer Ellison in the title role, comedian Les Buttons as Buttons, and with "Our Cilla" playing the Fairy Godmother.

The idea had come from her portrayal of the same role, the previous December, in Paul O'Grady's television panto—playing the evil Baroness had been Joan Collins, while O'Grady and comedienne Jo Brand had played the Ugly Sisters. *Cinderella* opened on 11 December and played to packed audiences at the Liverpool Empire until 4 January 2009, and was not without its share of controversy, not least of all when Cilla ruffled a few feathers by insisting that the rehearsals should not take place in her "home" town, but in London at the Old Vic. "A Lorra Lorra Hassle", screamed the headline in the *Daily Mail*, whilst a "spokesman" for the show observed in the editorial, "She laid down the law and said that she was not spending two weeks rehearsing in Liverpool."

In fact, this was *not* Cilla playing the prima donna. The behind-the-scenes staff, dancers and extras all were based in London therefore it was easier—and more economical—

to have Ellison, Dennis and the other leads travel to London, and their fault entirely that they did not take up First Family Entertainments' apparent offer to put them up at a hotel. The press harked back to Cilla's last pantomime at the Empire, *Aladdin,* when during the first show she had asked the audience how best she should kill the villain, played by Gareth Hunt. "Sing to him!" one wag had called out, bringing such a round of applause that the line had been left in. But if they were expecting poor performances on account of the disjointed rehearsals, they were in for a surprise. It was a fantastic production, with Cilla—at sixty-four—receiving standing ovations after singing "Step Inside Love", "Sing A Rainbow", "Something Tells Me", and "You're My World".

"Does it deliver?" asked the critic from *The Stage*, before answering his own question, "Oh, yes, and its thanks largely to the stage presence of Ms. Black who, after forty-plus years in the business, still knows how to hold an audience in the palm of her hand."

Then on 1 August 2015, Britain went into shock upon hearing the news of Cilla's sudden death at her holiday home near Estepona, in Spain. She was seventy-two, and had suffered a stroke. The previous year she had made the headlines when announcing that she did not wish to live beyond seventy-five, and suffer the way her mother had.

Cilla's funeral service, on 20 August at St Mary's Church, Woolton—where she and Bobby had received their wedding blessing—was broadcast live, and in full, on British television. Such was her importance.

She truly was unique.

Cilla Black: 1960s Vinyl Discography

1963
Fever
Dick James Music, unreleased

A Shot Of Rhythm And Blues
Parlophone, unreleased

Love Of The Loved/ Shy Of Love
Parlophone R5065

1964
Anyone Who Had A Heart/ Just For You
Parlophone R5101

Anyone Who Had A Heart: Anyone Who Had A Heart; Just For You; Love Of The Loved; Shy Of Love
(**EP**) Parlophone GEP 8901

You're My World/ Suffer Now I Must
Parlophone R5133

It's For You/ He Won't Ask Me
Parlophone R5162

Love Is Like A Heatwave
Parlophone, unreleased

It's For You: It's For You; He Won't Ask Me; You're My World; Suffer Now I Must
(**EP**) Parlophone GEP 8916

1965
Some Things You Never Get Used To
Parlophone, unreleased

Cilla: Goin' Out Of My Head; Every Little Bit Hurts; Baby It's You; Dancing In The Street; Come To Me; Old Man River; One Little Voice; I'm Not Alone Anymore; Whatcha Gonna Do About It; Love Letters; This Empty Place; You'd Be So Nice To Come Home To
(**Album**) Parlophone PMC 1243

Is It Love? The US release of *Cilla* with bonus song, Heatwave.
(**LP**) Capitol ST 2308

You've Lost That Loving Feeling/ Is It Love?
Parlophone R5225

I've Been Wrong Before/ I Don't Want To Know
Parlophone R5265

Poor Boy/ Shotgun
Anytime You Need Me
Parlophone, unreleased

Is It Love/ One Little Voice
Capitol 5373   (US release)

Please Don't Teach Me To Love You/ The Cherry Song
Parlophone, unreleased

1966
Love's Just A Broken Heart/ Yesterday
Parlophone R5395

Cilla Sings A Rainbow: Love's Just A Broken Heart; Lover's Concerto; Make It Easy On Yourself; One Two Three; There's No Place To Hide; When I Fall In Love; Yesterday; Sing A Rainbow; Baby I'm Yours; The Real Thing; Everything I Touch Turns To Tears; In A Woman's Eyes; My Love Come Home
(**LP**) Parlophone PMC 7004

Alfie/ Night Time Is Here
Parlophone R5427

Don't Answer Me/ The Right One Is Left
Parlophone R5463

Cilla's Hits: Don't Answer Me; The Right One Is Left; Alfie; Night Time Is Here (**EP**) Parlophone GEP 8954

Only You Can Free My Mind
Parlophone, unreleased

A Fool Am I/ For No One
Parlophone R5515

1967
What Good Am I/ Over My Head
Parlophone R5608

I Only Live To Love You/ Suddenly You Love Me
Parlophone R5652   (Withdrawn after initial pressing)

All My Love/ Step Inside Love (Parlophone, unreleased)

I Only Live To Love You/ From Now On
Parlophone R5652

1968
Step Inside Love/ I Couldn't Take My Eyes Off You
Parlophone R5674

M'innamoro/ Non c'é domani
Italian versions of Step Inside Love and Where Is Tomorrow
SIR 200080

Where Is Tomorrow/ Work Is A Four-Letter Word
Parlophone R5706

Sher-oo! : What The World Needs Now Is Love; Suddenly You Love Me; This Is The First Time; Follow The Path Of The Stars; Misty Roses; Take Me In Your Arms And OLove Me; Yo-Yo; Something's Cotten Hold Of My Heart; Step Inside Love; A Man And A Woman; I Couldn't Take My Eyes Off You; Follow Me
(**LP**) Parlophone PMC 7041

Time For Cilla: Abyssinian Secret; Trees And Loneliness; There I Go; Time
(**EP**) Parlophone GEP 8967

Your Heart Is Free Just Like The Wind
Parlophone, unreleased

The Best Of Cilla Black: Love Of The Loved; Anyone Who Had A Heart; You're My World; You've Lost That Loving Feeling; Love's Just A Broken Heart; Alfie; I Only Live To Love You; What Good Am I; Step Inside Love; Where Is Tomorrow; Sing A Rainbow; It's For You; Yesterday; I Think I'm Going Out Of My Head
(**LP**) Parlophone PMC 7065

1969
Surround Yourself With Sorrow/ London Bridge
Parlophone R5759

Quando si spezza un grande amore */ Without Him
* Italian language version of Surround Yourself With Sorrow
SIR 200098

Surround Yourself With Cilla: Aquarius; Without Him; Only Forever Will Do; You'll Never Get To Heaven If You Break My Heart; Forget Him; It'll Never Happen Again; Think Of Me; I Am A Woman; Words; Red Rubber Ball; Liverpool Lullaby; Surround Yourself With Sorrow
(**LP**) Parlophone PCS 7079

On A Street Called Hope
Parlophone, unreleased

Conversations/ Liverpool Lullaby
Parlophone R5785

If I Thought You'd Ever Change Your Mind/ It Feels So Good
Parlophone R5820

1970 (part-recorded 1969)
Sweet Inspiration: Sweet Inspiration; Put A Little Love In Your Heart; The April Fool; I Can't Go On Living Without You; From Both Sides Now; Across The Universe; Black Paper Roses; Mysterious People; Dear Madame; Oh Pleasure Man; Little Pleasure Acre; For Once In My Life; Rule Britannia
(**LP**) Parlophone PCS 7103

Kathy Kirby

The Way Of Love

Dusty had her trademark "panda" mascara, Sandie Shaw her bare feet. Kathy Kirby had the shimmering lip gloss. She was promoted as Britpop's answer to Marilyn Monroe: curvy, vivacious, sexy, blonde and beautiful. The eldest of three children, she was born Kathleen O'Rourke in Ilford, Essex, on 20 October 1938. Convent-educated, she never saw herself becoming a popular singer: with her crystal clear mezzo-soprano voice, her family hoped that she might have a career on the operatic stage and she grew up listening to this kind of music—her particular passion was Mario Lanza.

Fate would decree otherwise. In the summer of 1956, Kathy—then a pretty redhead—she had recently left school and was working for a local newspaper, a piece in which announced that the bandleader Bert Ambrose would be appearing at the Ilford Palais in the middle of a British tour. Ambrose (1896-1971) was the son of a Jewish East End wool merchant. A child prodigy violinist, he had gone to America at an early age, played with various orchestras before forming his own, and returned to London in 1922 to take up the baton at various venues, notably the Embassy Club, the Mayfair Hotel, and the Café de Paris. In the mid-Thirties he had discovered Vera Lynn, and had been paramount in the elevation of Anne Shelton to household name status. The advent of rock and roll, however, had brought about a dip in his popularity—as indeed it had many other bandleaders. Kathy Kirby would prove his saving grace. According to the legend perpetrated by her, Ambrose was halfway through his set at the Ilford Palais when Kathy walked up to him and asked if she might sing with him. He was so taken aback by her nerve that he consented. The song, "All Of Me", received such applause that she stayed on the platform and sang an encore—Doris Day's "Love Me Or Leave Me", from the Ruth Etting biopic of the same name. The meeting of these two giants, however, is now known *not* to have happened purely by chance. It was pre-arranged by Kathy's stepfather, who worked at the Mayfair Hotel. Not that this matters: what is important is that they did meet!

Ambrose took Kathy under his wing, and the pair are reputed to have become lovers, mindless of the fact that he was forty-four years her senior. This would be the first scandal in her life, but by no means the last. A domineering and unpleasant individual, Ambrose bullied his protegée into shape and early on in their relationship drilled it into her that she would never survive without him as her mentor. Kathleen O'Rourke sounded too Irish, he declared, so she became Kathy Kirby. He got her to dye her hair blonde, as *all* the blonde bombshells had done—Diana Dors, Marilyn Monroe, Jayne Mansfield and Jean Harlow. He told her what to wear, how to comport herself on stage, and initially what to sing. What he had no control over were her innate qualities as an entertainer: vocal technique, tone, range, sincerity, and bubbly personality. She is now known to have disliked him during the three years that she toured with his orchestra before it disbanded, yet she stayed with him long after their relationship ended, and he remained her aggressive Svengali-manager until his death, by which time her career had entered a downward spiral from which it would never recover.

Whose idea it was for Kathy to begin glossing her lips is not known, only that doing so completed her femme fatale image, to the extent that red-blooded males regarded her a vision of intense horniness, whilst the gay community adopted her as an icon, enabling her to swell the Elizabeth Arden *Victory Red* lipstick ranks already occupied by Piaf, Judy, Marlene, Joan Crawford and Tallulah Bankhead.

In June 1957, Ambrose dispatched Kathy to Spain where she spent the summer as artiste-in-residence at Madrid's plush, 600-seater Florida Park Restaurant. The next year, when not working with Ambrose, she sang with the Denny Boyce Band at the Strand's Lyceum Ballroom. By 1959 she had turned solo: Ambrose fixed her up with a series of engagements at the Astor Club, followed by a six-month stint at the Blue Angel.

In 1960, Ambrose assigned Kathy to the Pye label, and she embarked on her first British tour, supporting Duane Eddy. She made her television debut on *Cool For Cats*, and cut her first record, "Love Can Be", written by Clive Westlake, who would go on to bigger things with Dusty Springfield. This was very quickly followed by "Danny".

Both singles were orchestrated and arranged by Wally Stott (1924-2009), who later underwent a sex-change and became Angela Morley. Ambrose's suspicions, completely unfounded, that Kathy and Stott had become more than friends—and not the fact that neither these nor their successor "Now You're Crying" charted—were his reasons for moving her to Decca, in 1962. Her first recording session here produced "Who Knows" and introduced Kathy to Charles Blackwell, who remained her favourite musical director throughout her stay with the label.

Blackwell, twenty-one when he began working with her, was an arranger with Joe Meek, and would later work with Francoise Hardy, Jackie DeShannon, and more importantly Brigitte Bardot and Marlene Dietrich. Ambrose disliked the take so much—not so much the song, but that his discovery was singing with someone who he thought she might have been involved with, that he had the master tape destroyed. Kathy was however given the acetate, and held on to it until 2006, when it was given to Vocalion Records and issued on a compilation album of hits and rarities.

With Ambrose barred from further interference in the studio and winding everyone up, Kathy recorded Clive Westlake's "Big Man"—the story of the ordinary little man, the "bee in the hive" who does not stand out from the rest of the crowd, but who becomes ten feet tall when she gets him home, and in her arms. This was released in August 1962 and its follow-ups—Westlake's "Playboy" and a fabulous version of George and Ira Gershwin's "Someone To Watch Over Me"—failed to sell in large quantities, but she struck gold during the autumn of 1963 with her cover of The Shadows earlier chart-topping instrumental, "Dance On", which reached Number 11 in the charts.

Kathy performed the song on *The Morecambe & Wise Show*, and its success led to her being offered a regular slot in television's new live variety series, *Stars And Garters*, alongside newcomer Vince Hill. Set in a fictitious pub, this was hosted by comic Ray Martine—renowned for his blue jokes, he was asked to tone down his act once the cameras started rolling, but refused to do during the warm-ups. If this did not get the females in a fluster, the fact that the "waitresses" served their menfolk coloured water instead of real beer caused them to heckle whilst the artistes were on stage—a problem the producer solved, after several near punch-ups, by bringing in extras from adjacent studio lots. Kathy appeared in sixteen editions of the show, and recorded an album, *Kathy Kirby Sings 16 Hits From Stars & Garters*, the only one of her albums to chart.

In November 1963, Kathy reached Number 5 in the charts (Number One in Australia) with her cover of Doris Day's 1953 chart-topper from *Calamity Jane*, "Secret Love". Whereas Doris had performed the number in her velvety, sensual style, Kathy belted out the lyrics. If anything the flipside, "You Have To Want To Touch Him", was superior: it was composed by Kermit Groell, whose "How Wonderful To Know" had recently provided Joan Regan with what would be her last major hit. At the end of this year, readers of the *New Musical Express* voted Kathy Britain's Top Female Singer. The award was presented to her by Roger Moore—married to but separated from her favourite female singer, Dorothy Squires.

Early in 1964, Kathy reached Number 10 in the charts with "Let Me Go, Lover" (c/w "The Sweetest Sounds"), a US hit for Patti Page and, in Britain, for Ruby Murray. It was a song she disliked, claiming that she had been coerced into recording it by Ambrose. Later in the year she reached Number 17 with "You're The One", a veritable powerhouse performance of Elpido Ramirez' South American classic, "Malaguena", adapted into English by Marcel Stellman. In this, Kathy holds two Top C's for an incredible fifteen seconds. Her repertoire during this period was inspired, ranging from "pub songs" she had performed in *Stars & Garters* to exceptional readings of "Someone To Watch Over Me" and Peggy Lee's "Shangri-La" and "The Man I Love". Her version of French music-hall star Mistinguett's "My Man" ("Mon homme") effortlessly supersedes the one performed by Barbra Streisand in *Funny Girl*. She also recorded Bacharach and David's "Reach Out For Me", but Decca shunted this onto an EP upon learning that Dionne Warwick was to release the single. Cilla had kept her comments about Warwick to herself, Kathy had not. She almost certainly missed out on a hit when Decca "vaulted" her take on "Things I Want To Hear", which had been on the flipside of The Shirelles' earlier "Baby, It's You".

Also in 1964, after a season at Blackpool's ABC Theatre which saw her breaking box-office records, Kathy appeared in the *Royal Variety Performance* in a line-up which included Cilla, Cliff Richard and Gracie Fields: playing on her Marilyn image, she made a stupendous entrance on the famous revolving stage, emerging from a sports car. The following spring, she was chosen to represent the United Kingdom in the Eurovision Song Contest, held that year in Naples. Each of the six contending songs was showcased on her first television series, *Kathy Kirby Sings*, (this would be followed by *The Kathy Kirby Show* and *Here Comes Kathy*) broadcast at fortnightly intervals by the BBC (with a summer break) between October 1964 and February 1966, and netting Kathy an unprecedented £10,000 a show. There was Tom Springfield's "My Only Love", Leslie Bricusse's "Sometimes", Chris Andrews' "One Day", Tony Hatch's "I Won't Let You Go". The audiences' favourite was Les Reed and Barry Mason's "I'll Try Not To Cry". The viewers—500,000 of them, voting by postcard—chose

"I Belong", written by Peter Lee Stirling—in 1972, as Daniel Boone he would have a hit with "Beautiful Sunday". In these days before tuneless dross, silly song-titles and political voting, the standard or entries was high: the main contenders were France's Guy Mardel, who came third, Germany's Udo Jurgens, who won it the following year, and France Gall, who romped to victory now with Serge Gainsbourg's "Poupée de cire, poupée de son"—a big shock, for she had been booed while performing the song in rehearsal. Kathy did not accept defeat gallantly. The French press reported how she walked up to France Gall backstage and, whilst the other contenders hugged and congratulated her, Kathy—shouting that the contest had been rigged because *she* had been the favourite—slapped her across the face. "I Belong", which only reached number 36 in the charts, was Kathy's last British hit—charting low because Decca also released an EP with all six entries, which had charted at Number 10. The song was also a minor hit in Italy, as "Tu sei con me".

Kathy's next single, "The Way Of Love", was one of her two best songs that year—if not of her entire career. Written as "J'ai le mal de toi" by Piaf songwriter Michel Rivgauche for Frédérica, as "Parlez-moi de lui" it had been a hit for Dalida. Kathy's huskier than usual interpretation compares with "Weisst du wie das ist", Eva's version which sold over a million copies. She was suffering from laryngitis when she recorded it, though no one would ever tell and this only adds to its quality, the sob-in-the-voice emotion. With English lyrics by Marcel Stellman, Kathy's take was unusual in that it tells of how her lover has left her for another man. "Then what will you do when he sets you free, just the way that you said goodbye to me?" she asks. It barely scraped into the UK Top 50 because of lack of airplay by homophobic deejays, but it did reach Number 88 in the *Billboard* chart—Kathy's only hit in America—and warranted her an appearance on Ed Sullivan's *Toast of the Town* in May 1965, where she performed this and "Can't Help Loving That Man Of Mine." On the flipside of the single was "Oh Darling, How I Miss You", the signature tune of one of her *Stars & Garters* co-stars, Lynn Holland.

The other great song, put down as a single take on the same day, was "Where In The World", Ernie Dunstall's English adaptation for Dorothy Squires of a German song by Bert Kaempfert. Dot told me that it was about the break-up of her marriage to Roger Moore, which is why she often sang it on stage but never recorded it—giving it to Kathy at one of her famous parties. "Where in the world will I find another shoulder to cry on, now that you're gone?" Kathy asks, when so far as is known there *was* no love in her life, save that proffered by her fans. Kathy also recorded Piaf's "No Regrets", Charles Trenet's "I Wish You Love", and on a lesser note the theme from the *Adam Adamant* television series. Then there were the "sexy" songs: Clive Westlake's "Playboy", Earline Phillips' "Love Me Baby", and Otis Blackwell's "Slowly".

Kathy's star paled towards the end of the decade, and most especially after Ambrose's death in 1971. They were in Leeds, filming a guest appearance on comic Les Dawson's television show, when the bandleader suffered a heart-attack and was rushed to hospital. Kathy's song was "Come Rain Or Come Shine", which she insisted upon performing. Just hours later, Ambrose died, yet no sooner had he been buried than it emerged than in the space of ten years he had gambled away an estimated £5 million of her earnings. Trusting him implicitly, Kathy, who at the height of her fame had earned upwards of £40,000 a week, had lived comfortably on a weekly allowance and assumed he had been investing her fortune. Even so, for the remainder of her life she spoke about him with great reverence. Two years after his death she recorded a song in his memory, "Singer With The Band", in which she proclaims that she owes everything to the man who discovered her.

Ambrose's death and the aftertaste of bitterness, brought about by the fact that for years she had been associating with a crook, marked the beginning of the end for Kathy, who very quickly developed a reputation for being tetchy and unreliable—so much so that few impresarios wanted to book her. Not one of her twelve singles released between 1967 and 1973, nor her excellent 1968 album, *My Thanks To You*, made an impression on the charts, though they are regarded as much sought after collectors' items today, and Kathy's compilation albums sell many thousands of copies. Her final recording released in 1976—"He", a female response to Charles Aznavour's "She", is nothing short or remarkable and was one of several songs Kathy recorded for the President label, which had been instrumental for re-launching Dorothy Squires' career.

For Kathy, however, there would be no resurrection, no boy-band hitching a ride on the back of her name as would happen with Dusty, Lulu and Sandie Shaw—no television game-show to keep her name in lights, as with Cilla. The best she achieved, through absolutely no fault of her own and for no other reason than no one wanted to give her a chance, was a clutch of appearances on drossy television shows such as *The Wheeltappers & Shunters Club*, a coarse variety series set in a fictitious Northern working men's club. Here, Kathy put her heart into middle-of-the road ditties such as "You Won't Find Another Love Like Me", which hardly enhanced her vampish reputation—while the audience of mostly middle-aged men were only interested in peering down her cleavage.

In 1982, Kathy staged a hugely successful comeback, at

London's Lyceum Theatre. The voice sounded just a little cracked, but this was largely on account of first-night nerves. Even so, aged just 43 and still vocally very much in her prime, she announced her retirement after an acclaimed one-off performance at Blackpool's Horsehoe Theatre Restaurant. As such, British entertainment lost a living legend with so much left to give.

Kathy's personal life, in keeping with most of the great *chanteuses-réalistes* and blues singers, was rarely less than a disaster, with each pitfall or episode of erratic behaviour greedily gobbled up by the tabloids. At the time of her first television series, the gutter press reported rumours of her getting pregnant and having an abortion following an affair with Tom Jones. Other relationships attracted scurrilous headlines. Her marriage in 1975 to policeman-turned-writer Frederick Pye ended badly. Kathy lost a child, was declared bankrupt, and subsequently suffered a nervous breakdown.

In 1979 she was arrested for failing to pay a £300 hotel bill, and one of the bail conditions imposed by the court was that she receive psychiatric treatment at St Luke's Hospital. A regular visitor here was Sandie Shaw, who she had met in 1965. Some believe that Kathy's plight may have inspired Sandie—years after she semi-retired from the pop world—to found the Arts Clinic, a psychological health care centre for the treatment of show business people, not just stars but those working behind the scenes. She observes in her memoirs, *The World At My Feet*:

> Our paths did not often cross professionally. What we did have in common, though, was managers who had a penchant for gambling. As we were both under age Kathy and I would often find ourselves sitting side by side outside Crockford's waiting for our elderly mentors to finish on the roulette table....

Her story, which shall remain her own to tell, was enough to drive any sensitive soul around the bend.

Sandie, a Buddhist, taught Kathy how to chant. Kathy in turn confided in her, and once she had gained her trust, the hospital staff allowed her to take her new friend out for walks—with Kathy throwing the mink coat which Ambrose had given her over her fluffy pink negligee. These pleasurable little episodes aside, Kathy was forced to suffer the indignity of St Luke's for two months before the court order was lifted, though by this time the story had been splashed across the front pages of the tabloids—not only this, but news that whilst at the hospital she had received visits from a fan, Laraine McKay, with whom she had fallen in love and was planning to marry at the Chelsea Registry Office. The press went into meltdown, but the relationship ended soon afterwards when McKay was arrested and jailed for forgery and deception.

In 1980, Kathy sold her story to the *Sunday People* and observed, "The stage is in my bloodstream. If I'm no longer the glossy-lipped Golden Girl of Pop, I still have got one asset left—that's my voice. Someone, somewhere will surely give me that one chance I need."

Sadly, this would not happen. Such was her lasting fame that in 2008 a musical dramatization of her life, *Secret Love*, opened in Leeds—yet Kathy made no effort to go and see it, aware that they would almost certainly have got it all wrong. Then in March 2009, she gave her first interview in 26 years to James Murray of the *Sunday Express,* wherein she revealed that Ambrose's jealousy over a clandestine six-month affair with *Sunday Night At The London Palladium* host Bruce Forsyth—ten years her senior—had scuppered her chances of possible Hollywood stardom:

> Bruce was in love with me and wanted to marry me, but although we were very close, I still loved Bert....I discovered that a Hollywood movie producer was offering me a three-picture deal. They thought I would become the British Doris Day or Monroe. Like Doris Day, I was not a trained actress, but they said I could sing and I had presence....I think I could have played romantic leads or light roles in comedy, but my silly affair with Bruce had inadvertently brought it all to an end.

In the wake of this interview, it emerged that fifteen of her unreleased recordings had been discovered in an archive, and that these would be released on a CD—also, that she had been approached by the producers of *Desert Island Discs* to appear on the show. Kathy seriously considered this, but dropped out when told that she would be expected to talk about her personal life. Not long afterwards, having been diagnosed with schizophrenia, Kathy moved out of the South Kensington apartment where for some years she had shut herself off from the world, and into Brinsworth House, the artists' retirement home. She had been here but a few days when, on 19 May 2011, she collapsed and died of a heart-attack, aged seventy-two. She is believed to have wanted to be buried in Ilford—but if this was so, her wish was not granted and she was cremated at Mortlake on 1 June with just a handful of close friends, family and fans in attendance.

It was a sad end to what had been—and what should have remained—a magnificent career.

Kathy Kirby: 1960s Vinyl Discography

1960
Love Can Be/Crush Me
Pye 7N15313

1961
Danny/Now You're Crying
Pye 7N15342

1962
Big Man/Slowly
Decca F11505

1963
Dance On/ Playboy
Decca F11682

Secret Love/ You Have To Want To Touch Him
Decca F11759

Kathy Kirby: Dance On; Big Man; Playboy; Love Me Baby
(EP) Columbia DFE8537

1964
Let Me Go, Lover/ The Sweetest Sounds
Decca F11832

Kathy Kirby Sings 16 Hits From Stars & Garters
Let Me Sing And I'm Happy; I Can't Give You Anything But Love; Someone To Watch Over Me; I'll Get By; Acapulco 1922; Following In Father's Footsteps; Waiting For The Robert E Lee; Bill; Happy Days And Lonely Nights; Who's Sorry Now; Can't Help Loving That Man; If You Were The Only Boy In The World; The Man I Love; Miss Dynamite; On The Sunny Side Of The Street; Show Me The Way To Go Home
(LP) Decca LK 4575

You're The One/ Love Me Baby
Decca F11892

Kathy Kirby: That Old Feeling; Reach Out For Me; There's No Other Love; Shangri-La
(EP) Columbia 8596

Don't Walk Away/ No Regrets
Decca F11992

1965
I Belong/ I'll Try Not To Cry
Decca F12087

Tu sei com me/ Non piangero per un altra (Sung in Italian)
Decca F12088

BBC TV's *A Song For Europe*: I'll Try Not To Cry; Sometimes; My Only Love; I Won't Let You Go; One Day: I Belong
(EP) Decca DFE 8611

The Way Of Love/ Oh Darling How I Miss You
Decca F12177

Make Someone Happy: My Man; Happiness Is Just A Thing Called Joe; Body And Soul; I Want To Be Happy; I Wish You Love; Make Someone Happy; Old Man Moses; Sometimes I'm Happy; Havah Nagilah; Happiness Street; All Of A Sudden My Heart Sings
(LP) Decca LK4746

1966
Spanish Flea/ Till The End Of Time
Decca F12338

Adam Adamant/ Will I Ever Learn
Decca F12432

1967
No One's Gonna Hurt You Anymore/ My Yiddishe Momma
Columbia DB8139

In All The World/ Time
Columbia DB8192

Turn Around/ Golden Days
Columbia DB8302

The Best of Kathy Kirby: Secret Love; Body And Soul; Big Man; Shangri-La; Acapulco 22; Spanish Flea: Havah Nagila; My Man; No Regrets; Let Me Go Lover; The Way Of Love; Dance On
(**LP**) Decca Ace of Clubs ACL1235

1968
I Almost Called Your Name/ Let The Music Start
Columbia DB8400

Come Back Here With My Heart/ Antonio
Columbia DB8521

1969
I'll Catch The Sun/ Please Help Me I'm Falling
Columbia DB8559

Is That All There Is/ Knowing When To Leave
Columbia DB863

My Thanks To You: You Do Something To Me; More Than You Know; It Only Happens When I Dance With You; I'll Always Love You; I Wanna Be Loved By You; Thinking Of You; You Brought A New Kind Of Love To Me; If I Loved You; Always True To You In My Fashion; My Thanks To You
(**LP**) Columbia SX6259

1970 (recorded 1969) My Way/ Little Green Apples
Columbia DB8721)

Bibliography: Primary & Secondary Sources

Bret, David: Interviews with Marlene Dietrich, Peter Burton, Dorothy Squires, Marian Montgomery, Kris Kirk
Bret, David: *Doris Day: Reluctant Star*, JR Books, 2009.
Bret, David: *Gracie Fields*, Robson Books, 1995
Coleman, Ray: *Brian Epstein*, Viking, 1989
Black, Cilla: *What's It All About?*, Ebury Press, 2003
Black, Cilla; Barrow, Tony: *Through The Years*, Headline, 1993
Black, Cilla, "My Bittersweet Life With Frankie Howerd", *Daily Mail*, 1998
Davis, Sharon: *Dusty: An Intimate Portrait*, Sevenoaks, 2008.
Evans, David: *Scissors & Paste: A Collage Biography of Dusty Springfield*, Britannia Press, 1995.
Harman, James: *Kathy Kirby, Secrets, Loves & Lip Gloss*, Best Books, 2006
Herman, Gary: *Rock & Roll Babylon*, Plexus, 1982
Howes, Paul: *The Complete Dusty Springfield*, Reynolds & Hearn, 2001.
Katz, Gary J: *Death By Rock & Roll*, Robson Books, 1995
Kirk, Kris: Dusty Interview: *A Boy Called Mary*, Millivres, 1999
Leigh, Spencer: *Let's Go Down To The Cavern*, Vermillion, 1984
Martin, George: *All You Need Is Ears*, Macmillan, 1979
Murray, James: Interview with Kathy Kirby, *Sunday Express*, 2009.
O'Brien, Lucy: *Dusty*, Sidgwick & Jackson, 1989.
Rook, Jean: Interview with Dusty Springfield, *Daily Express*, 1985.
Shapiro, Helen: *Walking Back To Happiness*, Harper Collins, 1993.
Thompson, Douglas: *Cilla, The Biography*, Metro, 2002
Valentine, Penny; Wickham, Vicki: *Dusty Springfield: Dancing With Demons*, Hodder & Stoughton, 2000.
Howes, Paul: *The Complete Dusty Springfield*, Reynolds & Hearn, 2001.
Various: *The History Of Rock*, Orbis, 1982

Acknowledgements

Writing this book would not have been possible had it not been for the inspiration, criticisms and love of that select group of individuals who, whether they be in this world or the next, I will always regard as my true family and *autre coeur*: Barbara, Irene Bevan, Marlene Dietrich, René Chevalier, Axel Dotti, Dorothy Squires, Anne Taylor and Roger Normand, David Bolt, *que vous dormez en paix*, Lucette Chevalier, Jacqueline Danno, Hélène Delavault, Betty and Gérard Gamain, Annick Roux,Taylor, Terry Sanderson, Charley Marouani. Also a very special mention for Amália Rodrigues, Peter Burton, Joey Stefano, those *hiboux, fadistas* and *amis de foutre* who happened along the way, and *mes enfants perdus*. Thanks too to my agent Guy Rose and his lovely wife, Alex; and also my wife, Jeanne, for putting up with my bad moods and for still being the keeper of my soul. And finally a *grand chapeau bas* to Marianne for the beautiful music!

Printed in Great Britain
by Amazon